GUTTER POLITICS

CITY OF NAPLES 2024

Nicholas G. Penniman IV

No part of this publication may be reproduced in whole or in part, or stored in a retrieval system, or transmitted in any form or by any means, electronic, mechanical, photocopying, recording, or otherwise, without written permission of the author, except for the inclusion of brief quotations in a review. For information regarding permission, please write to: info@barringerpublishing.com

Editor's note—Errors and variant spelling in quoted material herein is reproduced as written.

Copyright © 2024
NICHOLAS G. PENNIMAN IV
All rights reserved.

Barringer Publishing, Naples, Florida
www.barringerpublishing.com
Design and Layout by Linda S. Duider

ISBN 978-1-954396-74-6

Library of Congress Cataloging-in-Publication Data
Gutter Politics: City of Naples 2024

Printed in U.S.A.

CONTENTS

INTRODUCTION vii

A LITTLE HISTORY 1
    Naples becomes a city. 2
    Election of 2016 4
    Election of 2020 6

THE MECHANICS 7

THE CANDIDATES 11
    Berne Barton. 11
    Tony Perez-Benitoa 13
    Bill Kramer. 14
    The "team". 15
    Garey Cooper. 16
    Nick Del Rosso 17
    Linda Penniman 18
    Ted Blankenship 19
    Teresa Heitmann. 20
    Gary Price. 21

THE CAMPAIGN ADVISERS 23
    Matt Hurley 23

Alfie Oakes... 24
Daija Hinojosa 25

THE ISSUES... 26

FORUMS AND ENDORSEMENTS 31
Out in front of the public 31
Council... 34
Endorsements 35

MESSAGING AND MONEY 37
Messaging... 37
Money 39

A BRIEF HISTORY OF PACS 42

PACS RETURN TO NAPLES............................ 47
Ted Blankenship 47
    Citizens Awake Now............................. 48
    Win America 56
Gary Price... 62
    Accountability in Government, Inc. 63
    Florida's Values 63
    Collier Citizens for Responsible Government 64
    Patriots with Principles........................... 71
    Realtors® Political Advocacy Committee.......... 72
PAC fund reporting 73

Heitmann... 74
Linda Penniman (redux)............................. 77
Facebook.. 78
Thoughts on PACs...................................... 80

"CHICAGO LITE" 81

THE RESULTS 87

ACKNOWLEDGMENTS.................................... 91

ENDNOTES 93

INTRODUCTION

☆☆☆

The sun rose on March 19th at 6:30 a.m.; the polls opened at seven o'clock. It had been warm that night but then the whole month had been that way throughout. The forecast was for 91° with a slight chance of showers. In some ways it made less difference than it might in prior elections because results would show that of the ballots cast, 44.5% came in by mail and 23.1% from early voting. Less than one third of the votes were cast on election day.

The turnout of voters in the City of Naples to elect a mayor and three council members was 51.9%, only slightly below 2020, with a presidential preference primary on the ballot that year. When comparing it to the 2018 and 2022 local elections the participation was eye-popping.

In the race for mayor, with three candidates, 8,565 votes were cast, 2,344 early, 2,880 by mail and 3,338 on March 19th. In addition, there was one overvote and 88 undervotes.

In the race for city council, with six candidates running for three open seats, the vote totals were similar in percentage terms as between mail, early and election day. There were 27 overvotes and 4,858 undervotes. Since three of the candidates were running as a "team," the large number of undervotes may have indicated a decided lack of enthusiasm for the idea.

Polls closed at 7 p.m. and results from the vote, categorized as preliminary, came in by 8 p.m., indicating a close race for mayor and also one close race for the third seat on the city council. Both were within 0.5%, so a recount would be needed.

This book is about the events of the March 2024 election in the City of Naples and details surrounding the campaigns of the various candidates. Behind the dry numbers is another story, one about the most contentious campaign in the history of Naples replete with lies, innuendo, misinformation and dark money. The amounts raised by some candidates was beyond any historical norm and was further fueled by political action committees (PACs), with a lack of reporting transparency and incessantly negative messages delivered by mail, text messages, telephone and social media. My intention in writing this book is not to cast people into heroes and villains. It is to simply lay bare the facts.

The story will, at times, take the reader beyond the City of Naples since some of the attempts to influence the election and some of the organizations involved were not local. There were no laws broken because the laws are written to allow, even encourage, the type of campaigning that has become so common in our country.

Reflecting back from the blessed perspective of hindsight, if all the mailers and messaging from PACs had never become a part of the election, and taking the candidates alone and by their words, it would have been a competition of ideas and solutions, conducted by thoughtful and decent people. With the PACs it became negative, nasty and contentious, with a focus on personality, not on the issues.

My wife was a candidate for city council. I was her treasurer and campaign manager. In those roles, I had access to people and behind the scenes conversations and materials that inform this story. Neither she, nor other council candidates with one small exception, had to endure the scurrilous attacks of the PACs.

In the tradition of good journalism, I attempted to contact Ted Blankenship, Gary Price, Teresa Heitmann and Matt Hurley to get their reactions and to give the reader a full picture from all perspectives. Teresa agreed to talk, Ted chose to demur, and the others did not respond, but I have tried to be fair by reporting their side of various incidents from secondary sources when available.

This book is written with the hope that this kind of campaign will never happen again in the City of Naples, but also as a reflection of a larger reality because what happened in 2024 is no more than a microcosm of recent elections in the United States.

To begin, it is good to have a little history.

A LITTLE HISTORY

☆☆☆

The earliest written record of white settlers in the Naples area goes back to 1874. Roger Gordon, seeking refuge from a storm, sailed into what is now Naples Bay where he camped on an Indian shell mound overlooking what is now known eponymously as Gordon Pass. He opened a small trading post, lasted for a few years, and then moved on to destinations unknown.

After he departed, a Philadelphia businessman named Hamilton Disston bought four million acres in south Florida in 1881, planning to drain the Everglades and create an agricultural paradise with its rich muck soil.

At the same time, Walter Haldeman, owner of the Louisville *Courier-Journal*, was chasing tarpon in the spring and summer and in 1886, with a partner from Kentucky, incorporated the Naples Town Improvement Company in Tallahassee, after purchasing 20,000 acres from Disston. They began selling lots, running along the Gulf of Mexico from present-day Aqualane down to Gordon Pass on a spit of land bordered by beaches on the Gulf side and mangrove forests in what would become Naples Bay. It was dredged and filled to be Port Royal.[1]

By 1910, there were 100 permanent residents and thirteen years later the Florida legislature incorporated the Town of Naples. The first mayor, Speed Menefee, was appointed by Gov. Cary Hardee along with members of the town council, all of whom had submitted names for office without election. Their job was to work with what was then known as the Naples Development Company.[2] The first meeting of the council took place on April 13, 1925, an act required to achieve incorporation.[3] Members were paid the magnificent sum of one dollar per meeting attended.

By 1934, elections took place with James Hamill winning the race for mayor by a margin of 47 to 6. He resigned four months later, and William Clarke was appointed by the council to finish his term. An unusual choice because Clarke was also town judge and a member of the Board of Commissioners for Collier County.[4]

Naples becomes a city

In May 1949, a major change took place. The council voted to amend the city charter and change Naples' status from a town to a city. The move was approved by the legislature; the new city had a population of 1,100 people. There was no legal difference between the two, but being a city seemed to fulfill a desire to be recognized as an important municipality and was part of a process begun earlier to create a long-range plan to provide public facilities such as a jail and firehouse.

City boundaries were clearly delineated for the first time and memorialized by ordinance.[5]

In 1950, the council decided to stagger terms, electing two members that year, two members including a mayor in 1952, and two members again in 1954.[6]

Another rewrite of the charter began in 1958 and continued into the following year. With the 1960 election, the job of president was eliminated and replaced with two council seats, bringing the number from four to six, not including the mayor, reflecting a sentiment that the growing city deserved broader representation.[7]

Naples, at the time, depended heavily upon the city manager for almost all administrative decisions.[8] In November 1961, another series of amendments to the charter were approved to increase the powers of the mayor. Until then, the main responsibility of the office had been to vote as a tiebreaker, but with the amendments was given a full vote on all issues. Administrative duties increased as the mayor would become the primary liaison with the city manager except when council was in session, virtually making any actions a final decision unless subsequently voted to overturn.

In order to attract competent candidates for office, the mayor's salary was raised to $1,800 with each member of the council being paid $1,200. It clearly had an impact because in the next election sixteen people registered for the open seats. But that was secondary to the good news that its chambers would be equipped with air conditioning.[9]

At that time, the charter required each candidate receive the majority of all votes cast. In other words, if 2,000 votes were cast, to be elected required at least 1,001. That was changed due to the complications created by having to print extra ballots to manage runoff elections.

One of the most unusual elections took place in February 1970 when candidate Charles Cox, former president of the Chamber of Commerce, filed as a candidate for mayor but in January asked that his name be withdrawn. It was too late because ballots had already been printed; fortunately for Mr. Cox, he came in third.[10]

Another amendment, passed in 2005, allowed the mayor to run for a second consecutive term overriding the one-term limit in effect for almost 30 years. That was later changed to create term limits by preventing a third term for the mayor and members of the council.

Reading the history of Naples, it is clear that for over fifty years, elections had been held with civility reflecting municipal pride in the candidates' qualifications and the fact that they were all neighbors in a small municipality. But that would quickly be altered.

Election of 2016

The first time it turned ugly was 2016 when incumbent Mayor John Sorey ran in a three-way race against former mayor Bill Barnett and Teresa Heitmann. Barnett was popular and well-liked, known to many simply as "Mayor

Bill." Sorey believed it would be a tough two-person race with Heitmann running a distant third.

Barnett relied on yard signs, especially along the heavily traveled US 41 running into downtown. The Naples Plaza shopping center from Mooring Line down to the end of the property at the Chevron station was heavily populated with his signs, put up on February 20th, alongside signs from the Sorey campaign already there. On February 22nd, an FDOT camera took photos of a person removing the Barnett signs. The person was hard to identify from the photos, but when Mayor Sorey showed up later that morning at City Hall, a camera there showed him in the same shirt as the person removing signs along US 41.[11] His explanation was simple and straightforward: "I felt like I had a competitive advantage by having that site and I didn't want those signs up there one minute more than necessary for people to see." [12] He believed that he had exclusivity for the location, but after contacting the property manager, it was unfounded. The incident, quickly named "SignGate," may have cost Sorey the election.[13]

The 2016 election set a record for money. Sorey raised $179,000, Barnett $118,000 and Heitmann a meager $19,000.[14]

It was marked by accusations beyond "SignGate," since Sorey had a contract with the Sugden theatre for $60,000, requiring him to work 40 hours per week, and Heitmann was coming off eight years of sparring with the city's manager and general counsel, fashioning herself as the outsider. It was a prelude to what would happen four years later, because the next election was equally contentious, with fierce rhetoric and the first appearance of outside money.

Election of 2020

Heitmann, after losing in 2016, came back four years later as the reform candidate. "It's time for a change" read her signs throughout the city. Mayor Barnett played the experienced and beloved "Mayor Bill" trope while enduring withering criticism from his opponent about traffic and overdevelopment. Heitmann improved her fundraising from 2016 to spend $69,000. Barnett, relying upon his normal cadre of funders, gathered in approximately $98,000. Heitmann won by a 900-vote margin, with 55% of ballots cast. Barnett conceded gracefully, saying that he was retiring after 40 years in city politics, and Heitmann was sworn in as the 30th mayor of the City of Naples and the 45th mayor since the town was founded in 1923.

The stage was set for 2024, but first we need to look at how elections are managed.

THE MECHANICS

☆☆☆

Elections in the city of Naples are now managed by an interlocal agreement with Collier County that allows the supervisor of elections to conduct polling of the residents.

It was not always so. A canvassing board, responsible for certification of city election results, was created by 1960 charter amendments. The board, consisting of the city clerk, a person chosen by council to serve as supervisor and the mayor, would oversee municipal elections. If the mayor was running for office, the council would appoint a substitute. The responsibility of the board was to tabulate all paper ballots, whether counted by machine or by hand, and to announce the results the day following the election. As the number of residents increased, this became unworkable and the interlocal agreement took its place, a change that also modified the swearing in of winning candidates because overseas ballots were given additional time to be received and counted.

There are seven precincts in the City of Naples. Each has a number of voting machines, depending upon the population, and is fed by hand once the voter marks the paper ballot. It is then transmitted to the supervisor's office and tabulated. As backup, and for mailed and overseas ballots, the supervisor's office has two high speed machines with an automatic feeder that can read 300 ballots per minute.

The entire process is overseen by the canvassing board, responsible for both evaluating the equipment before vote counting begins and for certifying the final vote count. The board now consists of the supervisor of elections, a county judge, and the chairman of the Collier County Commission. Since there are a number of judges, ten years ago a rotation system was put in place so a different judge sits on the canvassing board for each regular or special election.

Today, once the polls are closed, an initial machine count is electronically transmitted and posted by the supervisor of elections office. In 2024, since it was also a presidential preference primary, county precincts were included in the tabulation. With 67 precincts, all results had to be tabulated before the tally could be made public.

Once a preliminary result is announced, it remains unofficial because overseas ballots have ten days to be counted, and provisional ballots have to be assessed. Those are ballots where a voter fails to have a photo ID or, in the case of a partisan election where a voter disputes the party assigned by the voting records, or in a case where a voter argues he or she is properly registered and eligible even though not appearing on the precinct register, or lastly a voter whose eligibility has been challenged by a poll watcher.

Provisional ballots are not scanned into voting machines at the precinct; they are delivered to the Supervisor of Elections office and individually reviewed. The voter is notified and has two days after the polls close to prove that the ballot should be accepted.

Finally, there are the duplicate ballots. If a counting machine cannot read a ballot for some reason, it is kicked out and delivered to the supervisor's office where a readable duplicate is created by staff and reviewed to see if it accurately determines the intent of the voter. It's particularly true with mailed ballots because of coffee stains or small tears or damage to the paper.

According to state statutes, if a vote count is within 0.5% of total votes cast between two or more candidates it requires a machine recount. Preliminary results in 2024 showed two races within the parameter: the race for mayor and one race for the last seat on council. In the case of the city election where there were a relatively small number of ballots, the recount took place at the supervisor's office on Enterprise Avenue in Naples. The two machines, referred to earlier, are located in a glassed-in area immediately adjacent to a large conference room. Before the recount, the tabulating equipment is tested, and the canvassing board has to indicate there is no malfunction.

After the first pass, if the difference is within 0.25% or less of total votes cast, a manual recount of the overvotes and undervotes has to take place. An overvote is where the voter has marked more than the allotted number of candidates and undervote is just the opposite where the voter did not vote for the full measure of candidates. Each of the two machines at the supervisor's office has three bins. Once counted, the top bin receives perfected ballots and two in the bottom separate overvotes from undervotes.

Overvotes are normally tossed out as spoiled ballots because the intent of the voter is impossible to determine. Undervotes are more difficult. Each paper ballot has a series of little egg-shaped bubbles, and the voter must fill in the bubble for the vote to be counted. A check mark or an "x" will not do the job. If the total number of overvotes and undervotes is less than the number needed to change the outcome of the race, a manual recount would become unnecessary. Since in the March 19, 2024 election one seat was open for mayor and three for city council, four votes on a single ballot for city council would constitute an overvote and two would constitute an undervote.

Those ballots are then manually reviewed. In 2018, because of the number involved, volunteers had to be called in, but in 2024, it was done by the supervisor's staff. All recounts are, by state statute, open to the public.

We now turn to the details of the 2024 election and first take a look at the candidates for office.

THE CANDIDATES

☆☆☆

Five men and one woman ran for city council. Of the sitting council members, Paul Perry would serve out his term and not stand for re-election.

Mike McCabe, with two years to go on his term, decided to resign by Dec. 31, 2023, to avoid having to file Form 6, newly applied by the state legislature to city council members throughout Florida. Prior to 2024, local officials filed Form 1 to disclose primary sources of income, and assets over $10,000 (with no amount and little detail attached). The new form required that assets over $1,000 each be listed separately, and fully identified, as well as any source of income exceeding $1,000. McCabe was one of over 100 local officials who stepped down from their jobs in protest.

With McCabe's leaving, the council decided not to appoint someone to a two-year term but rather wait until the March election and let voters decide.[15]

Berne Barton

A native, Barton attended Naples High School and Auburn University earning a bachelor's degree in operations management. He began his career with Northwestern Mutual Life Insurance company, eventually opening his own agency, Arnold and Barton, which he sold in 2023 to NSI Insurance Group where he serves as vice president.

Married for 29 years, he and his wife, a schoolteacher in Collier County public schools, have two children.

He was recruited by mayoral candidate, Gary Price, to form part of a "team" that would run for council along with Price in his campaign for mayor.

Barton raised $89,111 for his 2024 campaign.

Tony Perez-Benitoa

Born in Miami, Florida, he moved to Naples in 2010. He was a familiar face, having practiced law as a trial attorney and mediator in Collier County for 35 years.

Perez-Benitoa had a strong resume from work with non-profits, including stints on the boards on Collier County YMCA and the American Heart Association. He also coached varsity soccer at Naples High School.

He was another member of the "team" and raised $65,710 for his campaign.

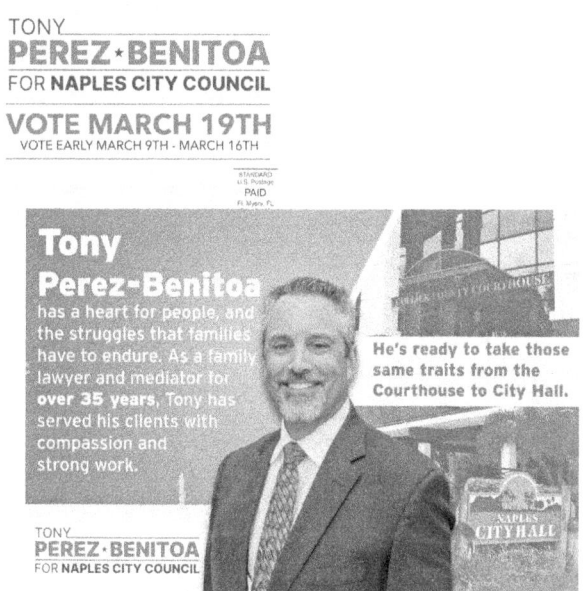

Bill Kramer

With a degree in health and physical education from Liberty University, a masters in computer science from Nova Southeastern University and another in counseling from St. Thomas University, he was the football coach at Naples High School from 1998 until 2021. Successful and well-liked, he was known to mentor players in more than just playing football.

Leaving his coaching job, he became the Collier County director for the Fellowship of Christian Athletes. He and his wife, a seventh generation Floridian, have four children.

He was the third member of Price's "team" and led the money race among council candidates with $111,750.

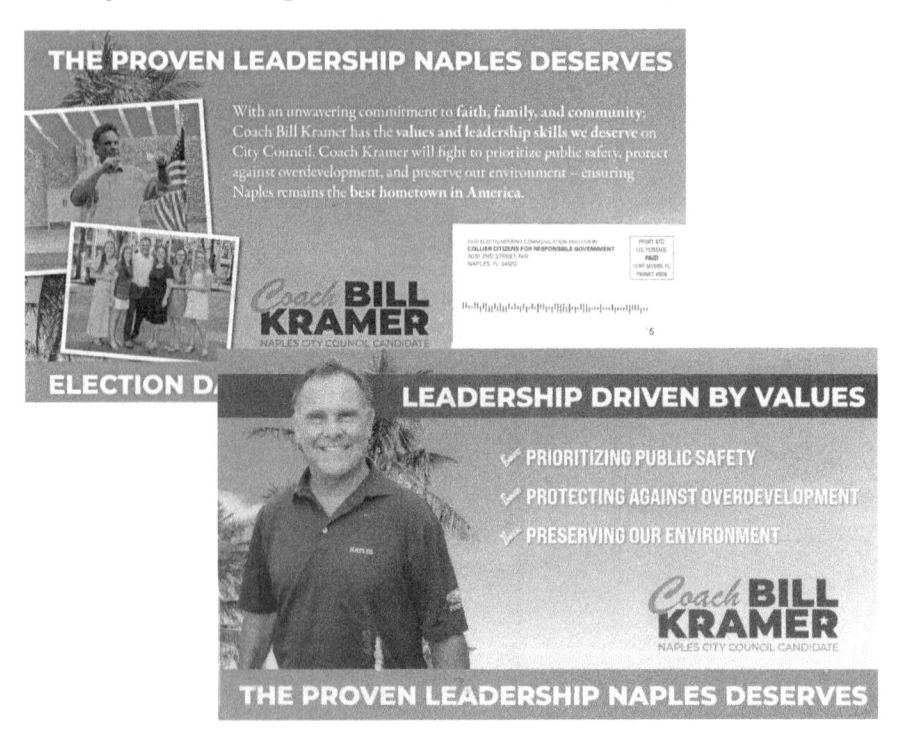

The "team"

Each member of the "team" promoted his own attributes designed to endear him to the voters. A mailer supporting Bill Kramer, whose name on the ballot began with the word "Coach," reminded voters that his teams had won two state championships and multiple regional and district football titles, and that he would spend his time on council "putting the right team in place." Tony Perez-Benitoa was always shown with his picture superimposed against familiar city landmarks. And Berne Barton always stressed having born in Naples and growing up there. The group also paid for and put out a series of flyers encouraging voters to look at all four candidates, including Gary Price, as part of a single bloc.

15

Garey Cooper

A graduate of Gettysburg College, Cooper had lived in downtown Naples since 2020, having worked in the real estate business locally for Premiere Plus Realty and later for Coldwell Banker. Before that his career was in a number of service-oriented industries.

In his run for city council, Cooper raised $14,610.

Nick Del Rosso

The youngest of the six candidates at age 28, his background was itinerant having lived in Germany and number of different states. A motorcycle rider, he had a bachelor's degree from the University of Virginia in communications consulting and work experience in asset management and environmental testing. He has made thorough and thoughtful presentations to the city council on environmental issues.

Running as an independent he raised $10,750.

Linda Penniman

A former member of the Naples City Council, she moved to The Moorings in 2000 and had served as head of the Moorings Property Owners Association and a member of the Planning Advisory Board. During her term on the city council from 2012 to 2018, when she resigned due to her husband's health, she served on the Coastal Advisory Committee and the Metropolitan Planning Organization. When she announced for office in 2023, she was living in Moorings Park and served as chair of the advisory board for WGCU public media.

To finance her campaign, she raised $43,900.

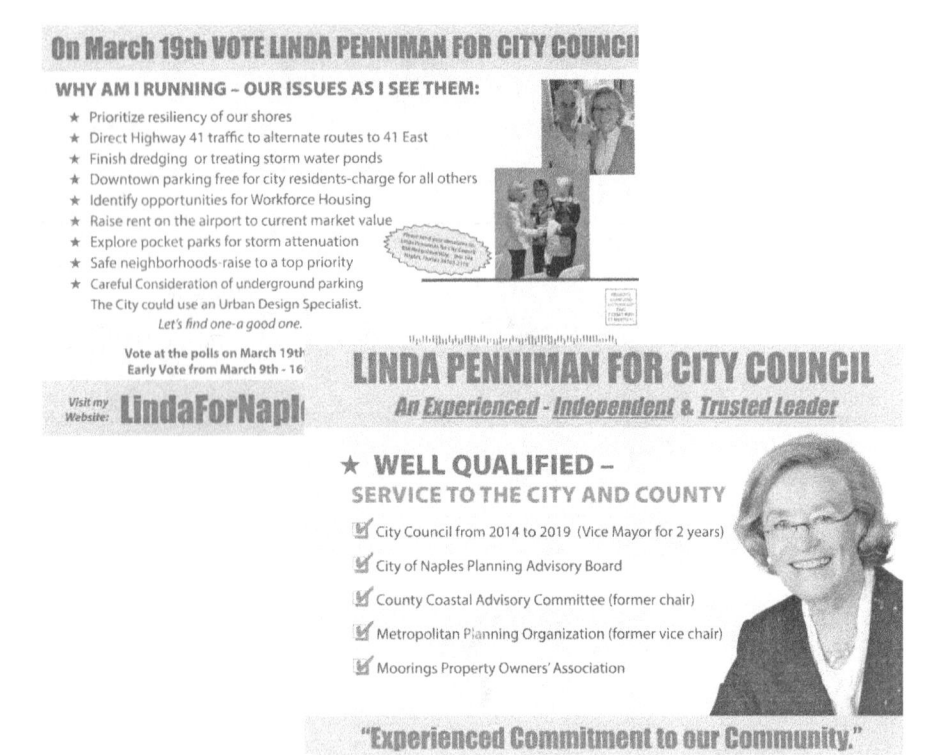

In the mayor's race, Ted Blankenship chose to not file again for council and run for mayor, Teresa Heitmann decided to run for re-election, both to be opposed by former council member and vice mayor Gary Price.

Ted Blankenship

Born in Talladega, Alabama, he moved to Naples in 2014 after a career as a partner at PricewaterhouseCooopers. A CPA, his work path took him through several companies as chief financial officer including a Naples-based InfiLaw System, described as an accredited for-profit law school with a focus on underserved minorities and students with lower LSAT scores.

Living in The Moorings, he ran for and was elected to council in 2020 as part of a reform slate and was known as diligent and thoughtful with financial expertise based on his business background and experience.

Supported by two outside PACs, Blankenship raised $87,572 in direct funding for his campaign.

Teresa Heitmann

Heitmann and her husband moved to Naples in 1988 where she served on a number of volunteer boards and as president of the board of Coquina Sands. Her business career had been in marketing and sales for a number of different companies such as a Lancôme and Revlon Cosmetics. In 2008, she was elected to city council, and served two terms until 2016 when she ran for mayor in a campaign against Mayor Bill Barnett and challenger John Sorey. Seriously underfunded, she ran a distant third.

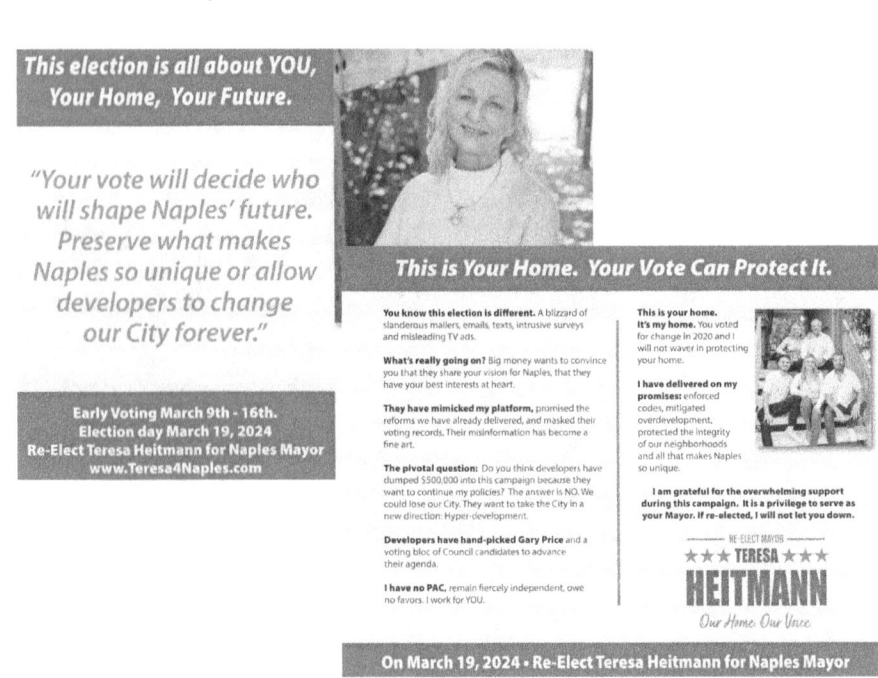

This election is all about YOU, Your Home, Your Future.

"Your vote will decide who will shape Naples' future. Preserve what makes Naples so unique or allow developers to change our City forever."

Early Voting March 9th - 16th.
Election day March 19, 2024
Re-Elect Teresa Heitmann for Naples Mayor
www.Teresa4Naples.com

This is Your Home. Your Vote Can Protect It.

You know this election is different. A blizzard of slanderous mailers, emails, texts, intrusive surveys and misleading TV ads.

What's really going on? Big money wants to convince you that they share your vision for Naples, that they have your best interests at heart.

They have mimicked my platform, promised the reforms we have already delivered, and masked their voting records. Their misinformation has become a fine art.

The pivotal question: Do you think developers have dumped $500,000 into this campaign because they want to continue my policies? The answer is NO. We could lose our City. They want to take the City in a new direction: Hyper-development.

Developers have hand-picked Gary Price and a voting bloc of Council candidates to advance their agenda.

I have no PAC, remain fiercely independent, owe no favors. I work for YOU.

This is your home. It's my home. You voted for change in 2020 and I will not waver in protecting your home.

I have delivered on my promises: enforced codes, mitigated overdevelopment, protected the integrity of our neighborhoods and all that makes Naples so unique.

I am grateful for the overwhelming support during this campaign. It is a privilege to serve as your Mayor. If re-elected, I will not let you down.

——— RE-ELECT MAYOR ———
★ ★ ★ TERESA ★ ★ ★
HEITMANN
Our Home. Our Voice.

On March 19, 2024 • Re-Elect Teresa Heitmann for Naples Mayor

She came back in 2020 to beat Barnett for mayor in an election that swept all incumbents out of office. Blankenship was part of that incoming group.

Heitmann enjoyed no support from PACs and raised $113,425 for her campaign.

Gary Price

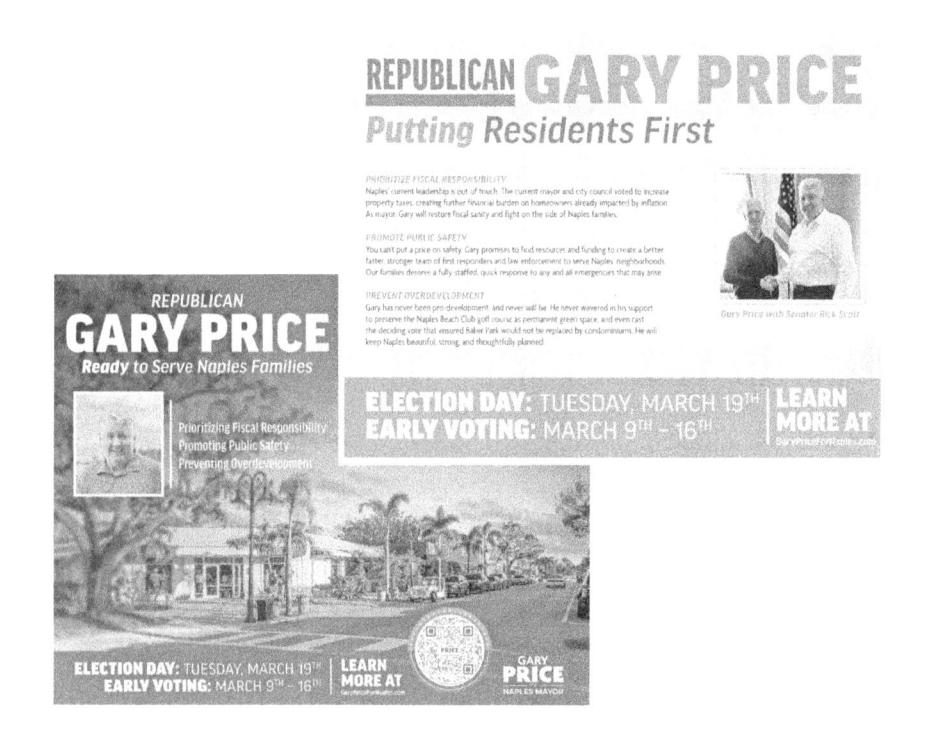

A protégé of former mayor Barnett, Price was a graduate of Ohio State University earning a degree in real estate and urban analysis. He and his wife of thirty years with their two children moved to Naples in 2001. He was appointed to the Planning Advisory Board and then to a seat on city council in 2005. He ran for office in 2006 and won election twice before being term limited in 2014. He ran again, successfully, in 2018, and then sat out the election of 2022. He was in business as a co-founder and partner in Fifth Avenue Family Office, a financial consulting firm, and chairman of the city's Pension Board for eight years. He is a licensed private pilot.

After looking at the clean sweep of challengers in the 2020 election, he decided to recruit candidates he knew would work with him and create a 4 – 3 voting majority on the city council.

He was the leader in the funding race raising a total of $294,217 and enjoyed the support of five PACs.

THE CAMPAIGN ADVISERS

☆🏳☆

Matt Hurley

As head of Southeastern Strategies, Hurley had a long history of collaborating with candidates and was known as a fierce competitor.

He had a number of business interests, one being the H2 Organization, a diversified company used for investment and management consulting. He also started Victory Insights, a polling and political strategy operation with a good record of predicting local outcomes.

In late January 2024. he issued a comprehensive report on the mayor's race with polling data showing a dead heat between his client Ted Blankenship and Teresa Heitmann. He went on to attack candidate Price with the comment: "Gary is often described as a hangover of the long-forgotten Bush-Clinton era of politics. His voting record, if consistent in anything, is that of being consistently inconsistent. His political positions change as quickly and as drastically as the beachfront tides, usually in line with the wills of his business client base, but rarely with the Naples electorate." [16]

Hurley would later become ensnared in a controversy over text messages being sent to voters saying that Gary Price had requested absentee or mailing ballots be sent to them. The matter drew the attention of Melissa Blazier, Supervisor of Elections, and was passed along to the Office of Election Crimes and Security in Tallahassee where it was never acted upon.

Alfie Oakes

A formidable power in local and state politics, Oakes was a farmer. In 2019, he opened Food to Table, a 72,000 sq. ft. grocery store that doubled as a gathering place for shoppers and Trump-style politics. He supported Ted Blankenship based partly upon his embrace of conservative principles and partly because of a shared a disdain for a decision made by the city to allow a drag show as part of Naples Pride Fest to take place on city property placing the blame squarely on Heitmann.[17]

He made a clean sweep in 2022 with his candidates for Collier County commission and in the school board general election.

Oakes had a PAC, Citizens Awake Now, used to openly attack Blankenship's opponents. He also operated behind the scenes by soliciting endorsements for his man from the Collier County Republican Executive Committee and Commissioner Chris Hall.

Daija Hinojosa

A recent entrant to the Collier County political scene, Hinojosa moved to southwest Florida in 2012, and had a long and successful career in various management positions in the fashion industry.

She ran for county commission in 2022, characterizing herself as an "anti-politician," with the comment "I oppose 'smart growth' policies and would never discourage urban sprawl. It's one good thing to be good stewards of our land and maximize available space, but it's another to chip away at urbanized living to encourage an environmentally obsessed agenda, all in the name of good will and affordable housing." [18] In that race, she ended up fourth with 5.3% of the vote, then opened a political consulting business and became Gary Price's campaign manager.

THE ISSUES

☆☆☆

Carefully framing issues is part of the traditional wisdom of how to conduct a political campaign. However, research shows that character traits tend to be more important to contemporary voters. One study described it thus: "One major factor is character assessment. Political scientists have found that, in deciding on a candidate's suitability for office, voters take into account, in the first place, their warmth, that is, whether they seem to empathize with them and operate with moral integrity. Voters also cared about competence—a candidate's knowledge, intelligence and overall effectiveness as a leader." [19]

Empathy—or the ability of a candidate to understand people's inner feelings and particularly their fears—occupies an important role. Playing on those fears with negative advertising tends to generate a stronger reaction than a straightforward recitation of policy initiatives which accounts, in part, for the growth of super PACs over the past two decades and not only informs the current political environment but also accounts for the growth of populism in the United States as well as in many other countries.[20]

The issue most discussed in the Naples election of 2024 was development. It was a major focus of Gary Price's campaign, who believed that the current city council was attacking property rights. Price's home, located in The Moorings and close to the coast but not on water, had been destroyed by storm surge during Hurricane Ian. He decided to rebuild on the same lot but to change the footprint of his house.

He had difficulty getting city permits for the rebuild plan, and in a comment to the local newspaper said: "Unfortunately, what I found was a mayor and council trying to change what we could build on our lot—instead of supporting our community, they worked against us. I realized then that my responsibility was to fight to protect all of our rights." [21]

He mentioned this again in a small private meeting at Moorings Park with a group of Republicans including a former state representative. When asked about the most prominent issue in the upcoming city election, he replied "property rights."

But that had not always been on the top of Price's priority list. In the 2018 campaign for city council, his issues were: greater public involvement in solving city problems, improving public safety, storm water management, and more careful attention to the city budget. Property rights did not make it that year.[22]

In the same 2018 campaign, Price, along with candidate Mitch Norgart, was backed heavily by developers, real estate agents, construction companies, and architects. The two were longtime friends of Mayor Bill Barnett who was known to be tight with the building industry, but Price deflected any accusations with a rhetorical response: "Is there been anybody with a longer track record of challenging developers in this town?" [23]

Price announced he was running at a private event on October 5, 2024, where he vented his frustrations with the city's reluctance to issue a permit despite the restraints on land use and development changes after Hurricane Ian with the passage of Senate Bill 250 which froze any local zoning or code changes to expedite rebuilding after the storm.[24]

He also talked about the loss of city employees over the past few years, arguing that micromanagement on the part of the mayor and council was contributing to a decline in morale among staff.

Harkening back to 1961, he suggested that the former model of a weak mayor and strong city manager would allow elected officials to focus on longer-range plans and push smaller decisions down to staff. He also charged that some meetings ran well past eight hours due to debate on small issues. Under his leadership that would change.

With his announcement, money started to flow. By New Year's Day he had collected over $70,000 for his campaign.

Ted Blankenship had been on the city council for two years and was always businesslike in his approach to governing. He announced his candidacy at an event in Baker Park eight days after Gary Price, echoing the charge that city affairs were being micromanaged by the mayor. His home in The Moorings had also been flooded and he argued that the council should remain focused on property rights and redevelopment rather than the smaller issues that he believed dominated council meetings.

He then attacked the possibility of an increase in the millage rate. Having served on the Pension Board, he offered a detailed explanation of the advantage of keeping the balance below a fully funded level and improving the overall return by slightly altering the investment strategy, a process that would make a rate increase unnecessary.

He played a slick video emphasizing his commitment to conservative principles, particularly regarding taxes. He agreed with Price on the failed attempt to revise rules on rebuilding, which he voted against, using the case as an example of government interference with private property rights.

Mayor Teresa Heitmann was the last the file, waiting until November 3rd to open her campaign at an event at City Hall where she pointed out that when she ran in 2020, redevelopment was an important issue. She affirmed her support of strict enforcement of the zoning code, pointing out that the more units a developer could squeeze onto a site might increase the profitability, but would lead to more congestion, more traffic, and parking problems. She remarked that it was only allowed through variances—which had been too easily given in the past and accused Price of loosening parking requirements for new projects.

She said the city was not off-track, and that she had dealt with two extraordinary events, one being the pandemic and the other Hurricane Ian. She vigorously denied council was micromanaging and took credit for hiring a new city manager, Jay Boodheshwar, as well as a new police chief and head of the fire department, crediting them with stabilizing the workforce and making Naples the safest city in Collier County. In response to accusations that she wanted to increase the millage rate, she defended her position that it was needed to pay city employees, particularly first responders, a competitive wage with a full range of benefits and even with a small increase, Naples would remain as having one of the lowest tax rates in Florida.

The candidates' presentation of issues at announcement events were always carefully scripted and designed to create voter interest and engagement. But there were other opportunities where the format was more challenging, and that was in public forums and endorsement interviews. In those came harder questions requiring unscripted answers and allowed voters to flesh out candidate's positions in greater detail.

FORUMS AND ENDORSEMENTS

☆☆☆

Another of the rituals in running for election in Naples was making the rounds of forums—some sponsored by civic organizations and others by homeowners' organizations. The meetings were used to inform voters as to how each of the candidates would handle specific problems related to their part of the city. Since the format was normally question-and-answer there was little opportunity to attack opponents except in opening and closing statements or after being fed a loaded question.

Out in front of the public

The first candidate's forum, at City Hall, was sponsored by the League of Women Voters and the Collier Forum Coalition. Mayoral candidates were a given the first hour and half and council candidates the second half of the program—all before an overflow audience.

As the question-and-answer session progressed, differences between the three became more about their views of the culture and management of council affairs than about critical issues facing the city. There was broad agreement on the need to recruit and keep competent staff, rebuilding infrastructure notably storm water systems, controlling redevelopment by adhering to zoning and building codes, dealing with congestion and traffic, and maintaining the quality of life with small town ambiance.

Gary Price argued that the council, under the leadership of Heitmann, had dragged its feet too long on approving new storm water outfalls into the Gulf, and a new Heart and Stroke Center for Naples Community Hospital. He also cited turnover among employees because of inept leadership and what he called a culture of fear. He returned to this line frequently in responding to questions but was never more specific.

In her comments, Heitmann spent most of her time on her record, her experience with the budget, the need to pay employees a competitive wage and the establishment of neighborhood plans within the city's comprehensive plan as the best way to preserve community character. She emphasized the need to address coastal resiliency given the impact flooding from Hurricane Ian had on many parts of the city.

Ted Blankenship, having served two years on city council denied there were problems with employee turnover then went right to the need to develop storm water infrastructure to deal with flooding. He took on the development issue by suggesting that the building codes be carefully reviewed. He went on to be critical of Collier County's approach to growth management, which had allowed significant development in the unincorporated areas near the edge of the city.

All three candidates agreed that the Naples Airport should stay in its present location and that the height limits in the city should be strictly enforced with Blankenship citing modifications to the original design of the heart and stroke center for the hospital as an example of the way in which the city, working with the builder, could arrive at an acceptable solution.

On the matter of workforce housing there was broad agreement that the city needed to cooperate with the county. Blankenship put a fine point on the subject, admitting there simply was not enough land in the city at affordable prices.

It was clear that each candidate was reaching for some way to separate themselves from the other two, because there seemed to be a whole cloth of unanimity about the fundamental issues facing the city for the next four years, and responses during question-and-answers remained genial and thoughtful throughout.

But that came to an abrupt halt with closing statements.

Heitmann opened by extolling her management of the city over the past four years, then pivoted quickly to say that 87% of Price's financial support to date had come from developers, builders and realtors implying that there might be an unspoken agenda.

Blankenship followed by commenting that the city did not want to return to an era of variances and fast tracking of developments, commenting that all voters should look carefully at where the candidate's money was coming from in an oblique reference to Price's coffers. "You're obviously taking a risk, or making an investment in their minds, for oversized development in the city, and that really concerns me." [25]

Price then quickly pushed back against his two opponents. Feeling the need to defend himself, he said that only 20% of money donated directly to his campaign came from the construction industry, real estate and developers. He went on to cite his vote against the annexation of Pelican Bay, his positions on green space around the Naples Beach Hotel property and support for the purchase of land for Baker Park as examples of his opposition to overdevelopment and embrace of the environment.

Council

Candidates running for city council all emphasized their personal skill sets based upon their work history and experience as primary qualifications for office.

Answers to the questions provoked remarkable unanimity of agreement on many issues. Permeating the discussion was the need for greater collaboration with the county on affordable housing due to the lack of available land in the city, and a strong sense that the overall relationship needed to be improved and institutionalized. Rapid approval of the hospital's Heart and Stroke Center, and cautious redevelopment of the Four Corners were broadly supported.

Strict adherence to existing city zoning and building codes was embraced by all.

It also produced some unique ideas. Perez-Benitoa brought up the idea of looking again at subsurface parking. Barton suggested a permanent liaison between city and County. Penniman argued that residents should be given certain preferences in parking. Kramer, part of the "team," suggested that variances, once granted, should not be considered precedent, a remarkable shift from past practice.

As with the mayoral forum, there was broad agreement on the issues and some on solutions. The conversation remained genial in tone as candidates all took the opportunity to focus on controlling redevelopment and preserving something called a "small town feel."

Campaign themes introduced by the closing statements of both mayoral and council candidates would eventually become what most people saw when they opened their mailbox or iPhones. But not all messaging was about policy. There was another element in the Naples campaign: the political action committee or PAC. And the messaging there was anything but positive.

Endorsements

Another ritual was an appearance before groups to seek their endorsement. City and school board elections were supposed to be non-partisan but Blankenship, with Alfie Oakes' influence, was endorsed by the Collier County

Republican Executive Committee (CCREC), a fact noted in some of the PAC mailers.

The Democratic Party was weak and disorganized. None of the candidates were registered Democrats so none sought an endorsement, and none was given. In Collier County a blessing from that quarter would be the kiss of death.

A second group, supposedly non-partisan, was the self-appointed Naples Better Government Committee. Headed by former mayor, Bill Barnett, a mentor of Gary Price, there was no doubt as to how the endorsement would turn out.

The third group was the Naples Board of Realtors® and given the amount of money fed into the campaign there was little doubt there either. Signs for Price and the "team" sprouted up all over Naples on the periphery of lots with construction activity, and in unoccupied homes for sale, posted by various real estate brokerages. The Florida Board of Realtors® jumped in, using their PAC to turn out two mailers in support of Price and his chosen council candidates.

MESSAGING AND MONEY

☆☆☆

In any political campaign, the most important decision is: who runs? The next is: what are the issues? And then: how to get to voters? Finally, what resources are needed?

Messaging

The Naples 2024 campaign was replete with all the traditional means of communicating including text messages, emails, mailers, and television and yard signs.

Gary Price was the only candidate to use television with a series of feel-good ads extolling his experience on city council and his interaction with neighbors. The spots, running on all local Fort Myers channels, tended to avoid in depth presentation of issues, using pictures with a sonorous voice overlay to convey a sense of warmth and empathy to connect with voters.

Direct messaging from the candidates, paid for out of campaign donations, was uniformly positive, filled with promises to "fight overdevelopment," "protect property rights" and "preserve Naples historic charm." But lacking was any definition of exactly what constituted "overdevelopment" or a detailed description of "historic charm."

Probably the most visible and enduring media during the campaign were the thousands of yard signs throughout the city. Every candidate used red, white, and blue except for Linda Penniman who preferred to use yellow, blue and green as she had in previous campaigns.

Signs tended to have static messages aimed more at name recognition than useful information. The theory is that mailers have a limited life that exists between the mailbox and the nearest wastebasket, and that in today's hyperpartisan environment any message that somehow does not comport with preconceived beliefs is quickly rejected. That's not true with yard signs. They have a longer life, are seen repeatedly, and do not necessarily go heavily into messaging. People tend to drive by signs, so only a few words suffice. Signs also tend to give voters a sense of how popular their candidates are as compared to others. And finally, placed in the right locations, they are the least expensive way to gain name recognition.

All the candidates had "meet and greet" events sponsored by friends and neighbors and businesses as one of the ways to motivate voters and discuss issues in depth. It was as traditional a way of campaigning as walking the streets and knocking on doors.

As an example, at a private event, this one in late February at Naples Airport sponsored by Elite Jets, mayoral candidate Gary Price along with two of the members of the "team," Berne Barton and Tony Perez-Benitoa, took a hard line about relocating the airport, arguing that Heitmann had been stifling growth and attempting to close it down because of noise complaints by neighbors in the flight path for takeoffs and landings. When told of the comments both Heitmann and Councilwoman Beth Petrunoff pushed back saying that they supported the airport in its present location.

As another new idea, Price commented in a newspaper article during the campaign. "Leveraging my great relationship with the Naples Airport Authority, I've proposed increasing their rent from $1 to several million to increase revenue and, in turn, ensure total compensation for our first responders and police officers." [26]

Money

The next chart shows contributions and expenditures by all six council candidates. With stringent reporting requirements during the election the final tally was due by June 30th and it's fair to say the numbers are a precise reflection of the candidates' finances.

CANDIDATE	CONTRIBUTIONS	IN-KIND	EXPENDITURES
Berne Barton	$89,111	$5,000	$81,625
Garey Cooper	$14,610	$649	$14,526
Nick Del Rosso	$10,750		$10,750
Bill Kramer	$111,750		$111,750
Linda Penniman	$43,900		$32,054
Tony Perez-Benitoa	$65,710		$65,460
TOTAL	$335,831	$5,649	$316,165

The differences between contributions and expenditures with certain candidates reflect either a repayment of the loans made to the campaign by candidate personally or in one case the creation of an "office account" where the funds would be used for purposes related to the duties of office. The couple of cases of money left over was given to charitable causes, notably in the case of Bill Kramer where almost $38,000 was given to three charities.

The next chart shows financial activities in the mayor's race. All three candidates had made personal loans to the campaign which they repaid reflected in the difference between contributions and expenditures.

CANDIDATE	CONTRIBUTIONS	IN-KIND	EXPENDITURES
Ted Blankenship	$81,572	$3,048	$77,559
Teresa Heitmann	$113,425	$820	$108,425
Gary Price	$294,217	$3,511	$284,217
TOTAL	$489,214	$7,379	$470,201

Taken together the totals spent on the campaign by the candidates was a little over $786,000, the most expensive in the history of Naples.

A BRIEF HISTORY OF PACS

☆☆☆

Before there were the super PACs—those high-powered, under-regulated forces so pervasive in American politics and in Florida today—there were simply PACs, also known as the Political Action Committees.

In 1944, the Congress of Industrial Organizations created the country's first such organization, to raise funds for President Franklin Roosevelt's campaign for reelection. That was the primary purpose of early PACs: to raise money for political campaigns. Sometimes they focused more on a cause than a candidate, but most often contributions were directed into races for the House and Senate.

For the first three decades of their existence, PACs—then associated most often with businesses or unions—played a subordinate role in American politics. Early PAC founders had no idea how much influence their organizations would later bring to campaigns.

Counterintuitively, the first major step in increasing their power came in 1971, when Congress passed the Federal Election Campaign Act, which, along with a subsequent amendment in 1974, aimed at reducing the influence of money in politics.

By setting stricter limitations on the size of contributions to candidates and parties, and by requiring the disclosure of contributions, those reforms initially seemed promising. But they ended up having the opposite effect. PAC heads quickly found ways to sidestep them by soliciting contributions of smaller amounts from a larger number of contributors.

In the next few decades, the number of PACs would grow exponentially. Before the reforms, there were about 600; by the early 2000s there were nearly 4,000. As the number increased, so did the difficulty of running for public office in the United States without significant financial support.

Over the next few decades, several restraints remained. For example, individuals were not allowed to give more than $2,500, but that would all change in 2010—the most important year in the story of American campaign finance—with the Supreme Court case now referred to simply as *Citizens United*, allowing special interests almost unlimited access to the political process.

The Court's decision essentially contended that corporations deserved the same free speech rights as people. The result was the effective elimination of all significant restrictions on contributions. Individuals, unions, and most importantly, corporations, could give however much they wanted, and the age of the super PAC had begun.

Those newly empowered financial behemoths were still disallowed from officially coordinating their efforts with any campaign, but the rules were murky. Many PACs were headed by former partisan operatives, intent on exploiting loopholes and working the system to increase their ever-expanding influence.

Many had little trouble finding the money. According to the Center for Responsive Politics, between 2008 and 2012 outside election spending tripled.

Candidates became increasingly worried about the possibility of super PACs swooping into their races with massive donations to their opponent and spent increased time appealing to wealthy funders. The more funders a candidate ingratiated himself or herself to, the more chains to pull when the campaign was in need of a boost.

While super PACs continued to expand their influence, public awareness remained low. In 2014, even though a majority of Americans objected to the idea that a handful of major donors should control the outcome of campaigns, less than half could correctly identify the function of a super-PAC.

Meanwhile, in the 2016 presidential election, super PACs raised nearly two billion dollars, and by 2020, that number was three and a half billion. Most of the money went toward TV and radio and printed attack ads showing up in voters' mailboxes, and in many cases, it was unclear who had funded them.

The relationship between super PACs and campaigns has become much more coordinated than reformers would like. Where PACs were once subordinate in American politics, today campaign finance reformers would contend: the forces behind them remain in the shadows and election outcomes can be bought and sold by dark money.

The 2020 Naples election saw the beginning of the PAC era in local politics with a group formed calling themselves Citizens Who Love Naples. The registered agent was Jim Rideoutte, formerly board chair of the downtown Naples Players and treasurer Bill McIlvaine, once a member of the city council.

Started on February 13th, it collected over $76,000 in two weeks. According to the local newspaper, "...(n)ine donations came from real estate firms, builders, architects or development companies..."[27] mainly from big hitters like Phil McCabe, major property owner on 5th Avenue South, Matt Kragh, architect and builder, Fred Pezeshkan, developer of large projects, and David Hoffmann, whose companies were rapidly expanding into real estate and transportation in Naples, and who reportedly wanted to turn downtown into a "...sophisticated Disneyland for adults."[28] Many of these would reappear in another incarnation in the 2024 election with a PAC called Patriots with Principles.

Citizens Who Love Naples supported a group of incumbents for reelection: Bill Barnett, Reg Buxton, Michelle McLeod, and Ellen Siegel. Advertising and campaign pieces were supported by Russell Tuff, a fixture in southwest Florida politics with a public relations firm and a number of small, niche publications.

The effort failed as a reform slate was elected including Ted Blankenship, Paul Perry and Mike McCabe. Teresa Heitmann won the mayor's race. But the PAC supporters would return again in four years, determined to create a working 4 – 3 majority. And they knew it would take a lot of money.

PACS RETURN TO NAPLES

☆☆☆

This was the case in the City of Naples election of 2024, when over $500,000 of dark money poured in. Because Florida finance rules are relatively strict, the donors would eventually become known, but PACs are only required to file reports on a quarterly basis and since the city election was on March 19th, any activity during the first quarter of the year would remain a secret until early April when reports were filed with the Elections Commission.

At least seven PACs were directly involved in the city election of 2024. Ted Blankenship had two attacking his opponents and Gary Price had five including one that sent out almost twenty mailing pieces.

Ted Blankenship

The first to work with the Blankenship campaign was Citizens Awake Now (CAN) started by Alfred "Alfie" Oakes in 2022 to supplement his growing political influence in Southwest Florida.

Having sued the Collier County Commission in 2020 for passing a mask mandate during the COVID pandemic, Oakes ran the table in the county commission and school board elections of 2022, backing candidates who agreed with his far-right politics and spending almost $80,000 in support of them.

Citizens Awake Now

CAN put out at least six mailers to selected city ZIP codes, all attacking Price and Heitmann as unqualified to serve. Oakes had to take on both, probably as a result of a memo from Matt Hurley of Southeastern Strategies, dated January 26, 2024.

In the memo, Hurley reviewed data from a November Victory Insights poll and concluded "...the race is a dead heat between incumbent Teresa Heitmann and Councilman Ted Blankenship. Price trailed far behind, barely reaching double digits." [29]

But the memo earlier made the comment that "...financial disclosures by Gary Price and associated PACs show that, despite our teams continued guidance and warnings, out of touch donors are, once again, poised to torch more than $500,000 in cash as part of a futile attempt to prop up a failed politician whom the larger Naples electorate simply has no interest in voting for." [30]

Victory Insights, of Fort Myers, another of Hurley's companies, had a sterling reputation as a good pollster. It had been used by Oakes in analyzing the county commission and school board elections and the two men were known to be tight with Southeastern Strategies, having been paid $38,750 by CAN in November 2022.

The mailers from CAN were varied in messages: three had a focus directly on Price tying him to developers.

GUTTER POLITICS

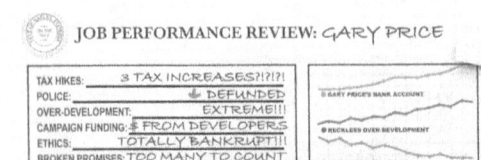

CITY OF NAPLES 2024

The attacks on Heitmann attempted to push her to the political left.

51

Other mailers dealt with taxes, a Black Lives Matter March, and one of Oakes' gut issues—initially allowing a drag show to be held on city property.

Citizens Awake Now wasn't entirely negative. It also supported Garey Cooper and Nick Del Rosso for council, as a riposte to the "team" that Gary Price had assembled. Another showed Blankenship with a pledge to lower taxes if elected mayor; on the latter was an endorsement from Naples Tax Watch.com but a search of the internet produced no such website.

Finally, there was one mailer billed as a "Voters Guide."

This provoked the ire of Melissa Blazier, Collier County Supervisor of Elections who, in an interview made this point: "We had a problem with Matt Hurley when something called the 2024 Voters' Guide was mailed without our permission or knowledge. The election code states that we are the only

CITY OF NAPLES 2024

agency permitted to distribute voter guides. My working life lies in Chapter 106 of the Florida Election Code. I practically know it by heart, and this is a violation of code." [31]

55

Hurley seemed to be the center of Blazier's concerns. He was tied in with another PAC that supported Ted Blankenship called Win America, started by Marlon Bruce.

Win America

Born in Brooklyn and moving to Florida in 2011, Bruce, after graduating high school, moved to Gainesville and attended Santa Fe College where he ran into some difficulties for allegedly voting in a Democratic primary in a district, he didn't live in. At Santa Fe, he was vice president of Young Americans for Liberty and associated with the campaign of state representative Charles "Chuck" Clemons, a Republican who would later become speaker of the Florida House. In the same year he ran for mayor of Gainesville, coming in last in a four-person race. He started the PAC in February 2021 and in August, with a clever play on words, a real estate business called Win America Unlimited.

Coming into the 2024 city election, the treasurer of Win America was William Stafford Jones. A fixture in the world of Florida PACs, he had spawned dozens and was able to move large amounts money around quickly. The registered agent was Richard Coates, a Tallahassee lawyer and one time counsel of the Florida Republican party.

Jones had poked into city elections in Martin County in 2018, supporting Republican candidates using derogatory mailers against opponents, but was relatively unknown in Collier County until early February when a volcanic scandal erupted.

With only six weeks to go, Supervisor Blazier received an email from a woman who reported receiving a text message that Gary Price had requested a mail ballot on her behalf. Blazier was concerned but needed further proof; the woman took a screenshot of the message and sent it.

Then the calls and emails began to flood in. The same message had been sent to a number of other voters in the city. The supervisor's office had to become involved because in the normal course of politics such messages, although false, were simply considered part of the cacophony of politics. But in this case, where the complaint was directed to a registered voter, she felt it gave the supervisor's office a reason to assert jurisdiction.

Gathering information on the messages, Blazier discovered that the posts had come from Win America in an attempt to discredit Price. Blazier believed it was blatant fraud and, after receiving assurance that they would look into the matter immediately, turned the information over to the Office of Election Crimes and Security in Tallahassee, better known as Florida's Election Police. Her comment to a local television station was, "I think that's why in the end I decided we should get involved because yes, if you look at what is happening now in a small municipal election, I can only imagine what's going to happen in November." [32]

Price agreed: "I think voters have lost a lot of confidence and that is one of the things I think we need to preserve. The people need to feel comfortable with their election regardless of the outcome." [33]

However, the matter still lies on someone's desk at the Office of Election Crimes in Tallahassee.

Reflecting back on the incident, Blazier said: "With regard to the Win America PAC, Stafford Jones is a good manager. He plays by the rules. You may not like what he does because he does play hardball but at least he stayed within the guard rails. In the current election in the city, I think Matt Hurley somehow pulled one of Jones's PACs into the mix because it was run by some youngsters who had no idea what they were doing. I know Stafford and when I talked with him about it, he said 'I can't believe that we got dragged into this.'" [34]

As a result, Jones took his name off as treasurer of the PAC within 24 hours and sent an email to Republican Party members: "The PAC was originally set up by some young people, and when they got into trouble with it, Coates and I dug them out. It seems that the chairman of Win America, unbeknownst to me, got involved in your mayoral election, working with Matt Hurley. Texts went out from the PAC to voters that hadn't requested an absentee ballot." [35]

Hurley categorically denied any connection with the PAC in an email to the : "You would have to ask their folks about specifics on their outreach and campaign tactics." [36]

The PAC had other ways to play the game. A mailer sent only to registered Democrats in the city trumpeted that Heitmann was adamantly anti-abortion and stood with Governor DeSantis in his stance on the matter. The piece showed a picture of the two of them, but Heitmann said she had never been photographed with the governor and commented: "I have never shared my personal opinion on this issue, ever. The private issue has no place in our city governance." [37]

After Jones and Coates resigned, the mailing and reporting address for the PAC changed from 1722 NW. 80th Blvd. to NW. 5th Pl. in Gainesville. During the election, it distributed four mailers all attacking Gary Price. The first two, from the earlier address called him the ultimate DeSantis antagonist; another cited an article from the local paper that he had voted to defund the Naples police department.

GUTTER POLITICS

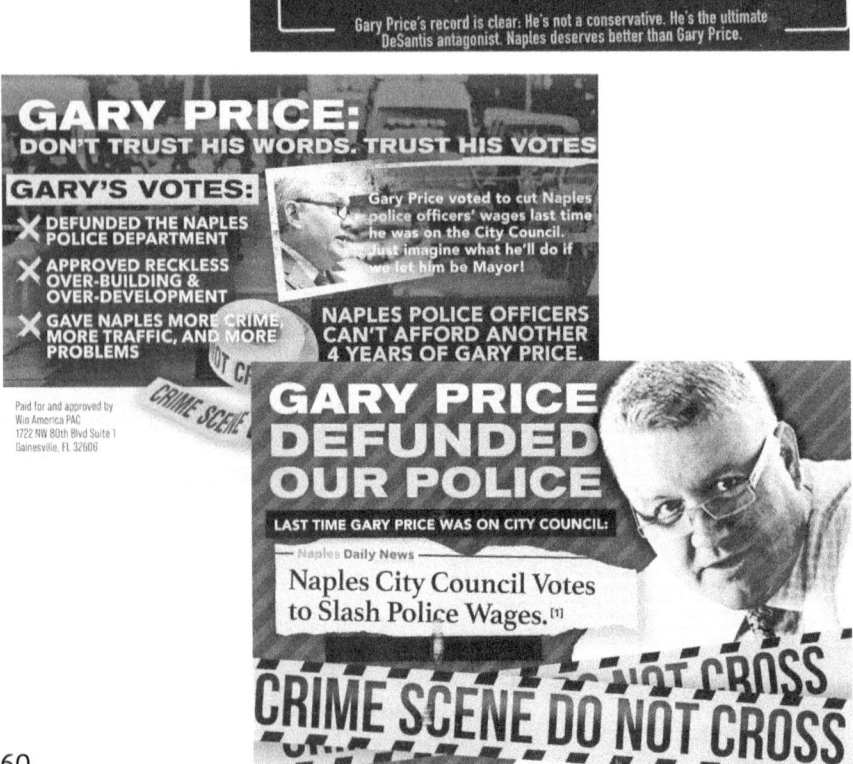

CITY OF NAPLES 2024

After the address shift a new mailer showed a picture of Price with President Biden and the headline "Weak Men Create Hard Times."

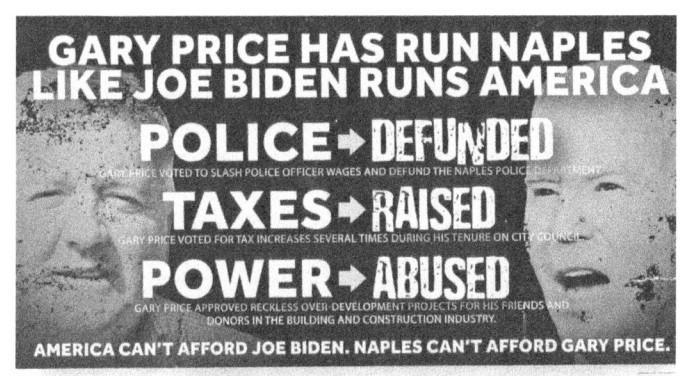

GARY PRICE HAS RUN NAPLES LIKE JOE BIDEN RUNS AMERICA
POLICE → DEFUNDED
GARY PRICE VOTED TO SLASH POLICE OFFICER WAGES AND DEFUND THE NAPLES POLICE DEPARTMENT
TAXES → RAISED
GARY PRICE VOTED FOR TAX INCREASES SEVERAL TIMES DURING HIS TENURE ON CITY COUNCIL
POWER → ABUSED
GARY PRICE APPROVED RECKLESS OVER-DEVELOPMENT PROJECTS FOR HIS FRIENDS AND DONORS IN THE BUILDING AND CONSTRUCTION INDUSTRY.
AMERICA CAN'T AFFORD JOE BIDEN. NAPLES CAN'T AFFORD GARY PRICE.

Paid disclaimer responsible for by
Win America
7600 NW 5th PL
Gainesville, FL 32607

WEAK MEN CREATE HARD TIMES

And just to rub a little salt into the wound another mailer showed Gary Price and candidate Bill Kramer, the popular Naples High football coach, together with the headline "birds of a feather flock together; developers are destroying Naples." The address may have changed but the message remained.

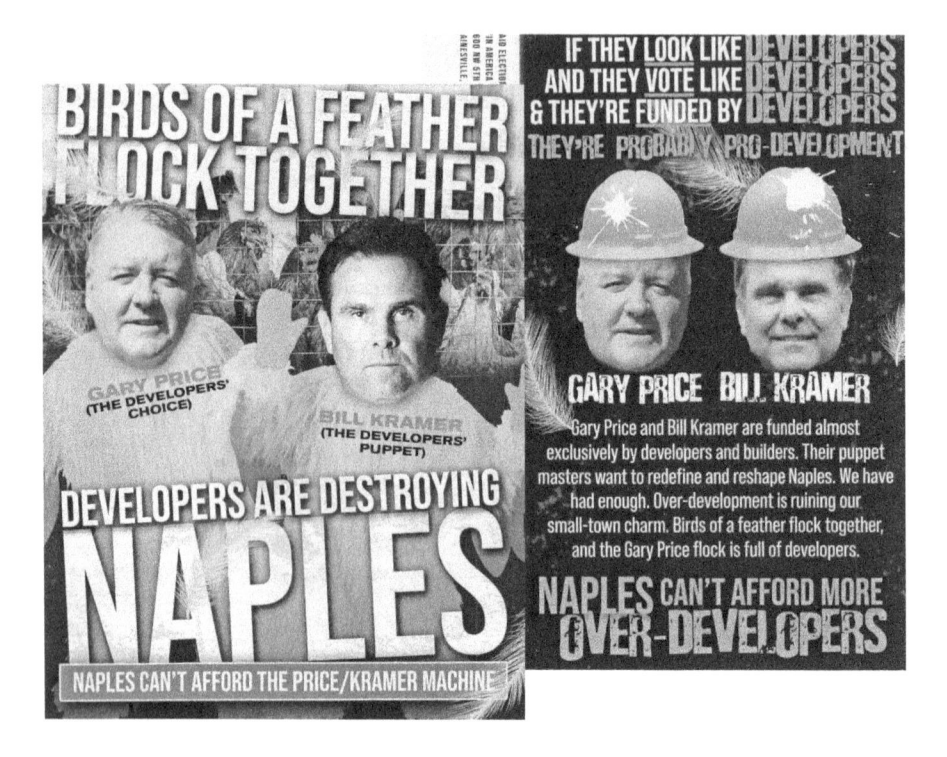

In response to questions from the media, the PAC's attorney Kristina Heuser stonewalled. "Mr. Hurley is not a Win America vendor."[38] She then doubled down: "Win America PAC has in no way misled any voters in Naples. Mr. Jones is not associated with Win America and has zero authority to speak on its behalf, nor any knowledge of outreach, past, present, or future."[39]

Blazier's final comment summed it up: "This is simply the work of one person who doesn't play by the rules."

Gary Price

Gary Price had five PACs working over his opponents and extolling his virtues.

Accountability in Government, Inc.

In a somewhat curious coincidence, another PAC, this one run by the ubiquitous Stafford Jones, chimed in with another "birds of a feather" mailer, this one arriving in mailboxes on March 1st, blaring that Blankenship and Heitmann were "unethical, shady, misleading."

Florida's Values

Almost a mimic of the Accountability in Government piece another Stafford Jones PAC, Florida's Values, mailed out a piece saying "Blankenship's Consultant Accused Of Confusing Voters With Bogus Text Messages," accompanied by a mug shot of Matt Hurley, in an obvious reference to the earlier flap over mail ballot requests referred to the Election Police in Tallahassee. It also reiterated the charge that the state Ethics Commission found that Heitmann had abused her power as mayor by hiring outside counsel to pursue charges of office and personal computer hacking. The finding was on a thin edge and eventually dropped.

Collier Citizens for Responsible Government

The heavyweight was Collier Citizens for Responsible Government. Starting in October 2024, just six days after Price announced his candidacy, it was headed by Miles Scofield, a fourth generation Floridian with farming operations near Immokalee and owner of a marine consulting company.

Fundraising ramped up in January with over $160,000 collected from local luminaries like Robert and Barbara Crown, owners of a group of wireless towers throughout the country, Jay Hartington, owner of Marissa Collections, and Peter Gilgan, CEO of Mattamy Homes, builder of mansions across Canada and the U.S. All lived in Port Royal, where Gilgan had just finished a 32,000 sq. ft. home using geothermal cooling and solar to attempt to reach an energy consumption level of net zero. Together, the three families accounted for $90,000 to the PAC.

TM Strategic Consulting was the biggest beneficiary, receiving over $104,000 for mailers and consulting services. Owned by Terry Miller of Cape Coral, it had a number of Republican candidates for the Florida House and Senate as clients. The company's profile was raised in 2019 when Matt Caldwell, former state representative and candidate for Agriculture Commissioner joined the firm as a partner after losing to Nikki Fried in the 2018 election.

In the Naples campaign, the mailers took on Blankenship and Heitmann as being big spenders, as responding weakly to Hurricane Ian, failing to move the storm water outfall project forward, and increasing traffic with overdevelopment. The series always began Teresa + Ted = .

GUTTER POLITICS

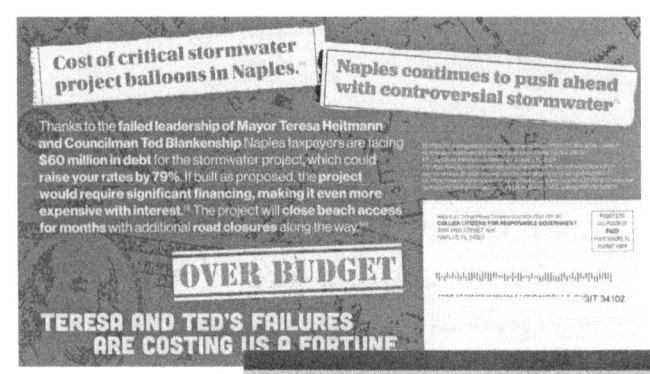

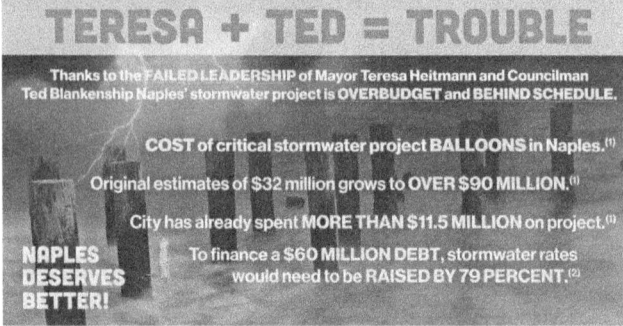

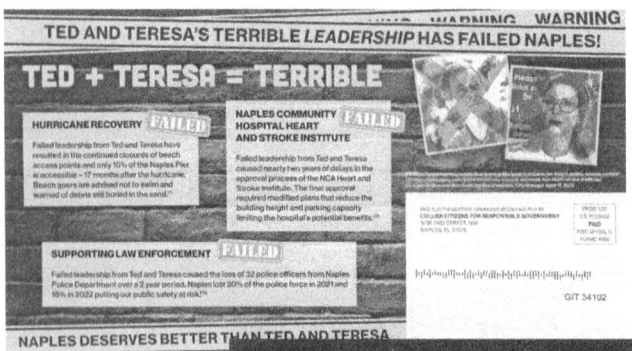

CITY OF NAPLES 2024

GUTTER POLITICS

To nearly orchestrated perfection, each of those themes was repeated again and again by Price in his public appearances and interviews, assuring voters he would deal with each of the problems either left undone or somehow mismanaged by the two during their terms on city council.

Going beyond issues, one flyer appearing in mailboxes on March 4th, vaguely placed blame on Blankenship for causing the resignation of 32 police officers putting public safety in the city at risk.

Ted Blankenship Seems to Only Care About Law Enforcement When It's an Election Year.

Ted's failed leadership caused the loss of 32 police officers over a 2 year period. Naples lost 20% of the police force in 2021 and 16% in 2022 putting our public safety at risk![3]

"Many of the new hires are young and inexperienced, or still in the academy, so they're not yet working at their full potential."[4]

"The city was losing employees as fast as it could fill open slots, including police officers, prompting community concerns about safety."[4]

Ted Blankenship's campaign wants you to believe he supports law enforcement, but that is NOT his record on City Council!

Police officers in Naples are upset after they say city leaders went back on an agreement on a new labor contract.

"We're seeing crime rates go up. We are trying to stay on top of it the best we can. We've had to close specialty units and have personnel work double duty," says Naples Police Sergeant.[2]

The city council met in a closed-doors executive session and rescinded the deal.[0]

Naples Police is suffering a 20 percent staffing shortage because of a lack of competitive pay and benefits.[2]

The Naples police pay is 15 to 20 percent less than the average for other police departments in the state.[3]

"Even though the city has not necessarily negotiated in good faith, our officers continue to do their best and give 110% to the residents."[1]

To balance the accusations against Blankenship the PAC produced a flyer excoriating Heitmann for delaying approval of the NCH Heart and Stroke Center, for closing beaches and the pier, and repeating the charge that she misused her power as mayor, an issue that would appear in detail.

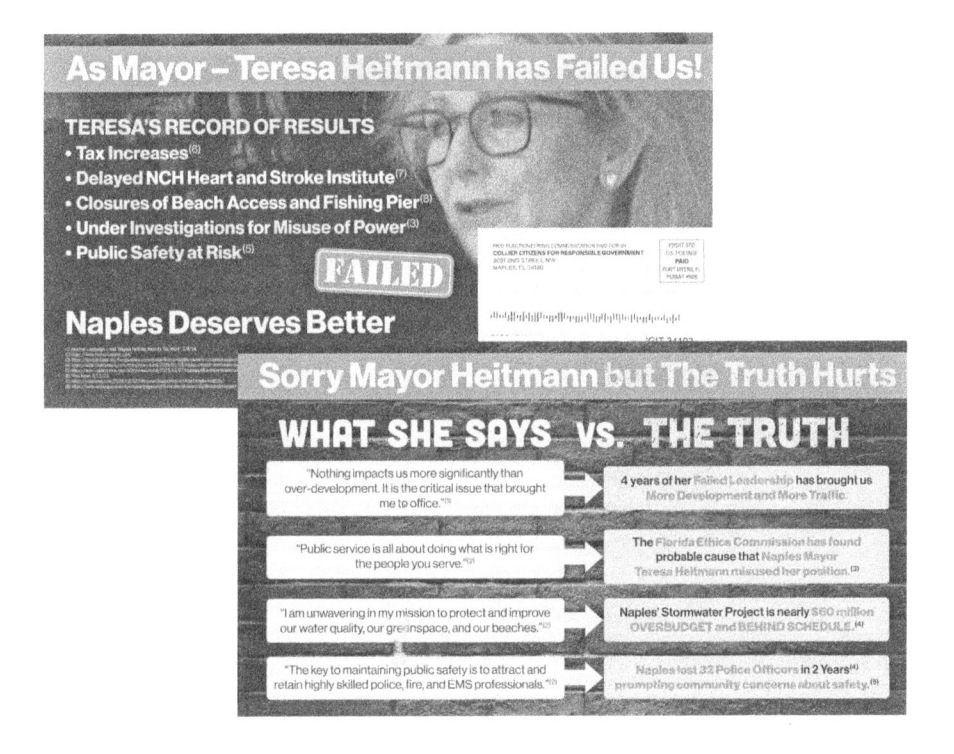

As Mayor – Teresa Heitmann has Failed Us!

TERESA'S RECORD OF RESULTS
- Tax Increases[6]
- Delayed NCH Heart and Stroke Institute[7]
- Closures of Beach Access and Fishing Pier[8]
- Under Investigations for Misuse of Power[3]
- Public Safety at Risk[5]

FAILED

Naples Deserves Better

Sorry Mayor Heitmann but The Truth Hurts

WHAT SHE SAYS VS. THE TRUTH

"Nothing impacts us more significantly than over-development. It is the critical issue that brought me to office."[1]	4 years of her Failed Leadership has brought us More Development and More Traffic.
"Public service is all about doing what is right for the people you serve."[2]	The Florida Ethics Commission has found probable cause that Naples Mayor Teresa Heitmann misused her position.[3]
"I am unwavering in my mission to protect and improve our water quality, our greenspace, and our beaches."[10]	Naples' Stormwater Project is nearly $60 million OVERBUDGET and BEHIND SCHEDULE.[4]
"The key to maintaining public safety is to attract and retain highly skilled police, fire, and EMS professionals."[5]	Naples lost 32 Police Officers in 2 Years[4] prompting community concerns about safety.[5]

Another mailer dredged up an investigation by the Florida Commission on Ethics into Heitmann's activities as mayor. Originally filed by Brian Dye, director of technology services for the city with the newly formed Naples Ethics Commission, it alleged that she used city funds to hire an outside attorney to get a legal opinion on how to deal with possible personal computer hacks by the city attorney or his law firm, and that she had given Dye instructions to take actions he regarded as illegal and possibly criminal.

GUTTER POLITICS

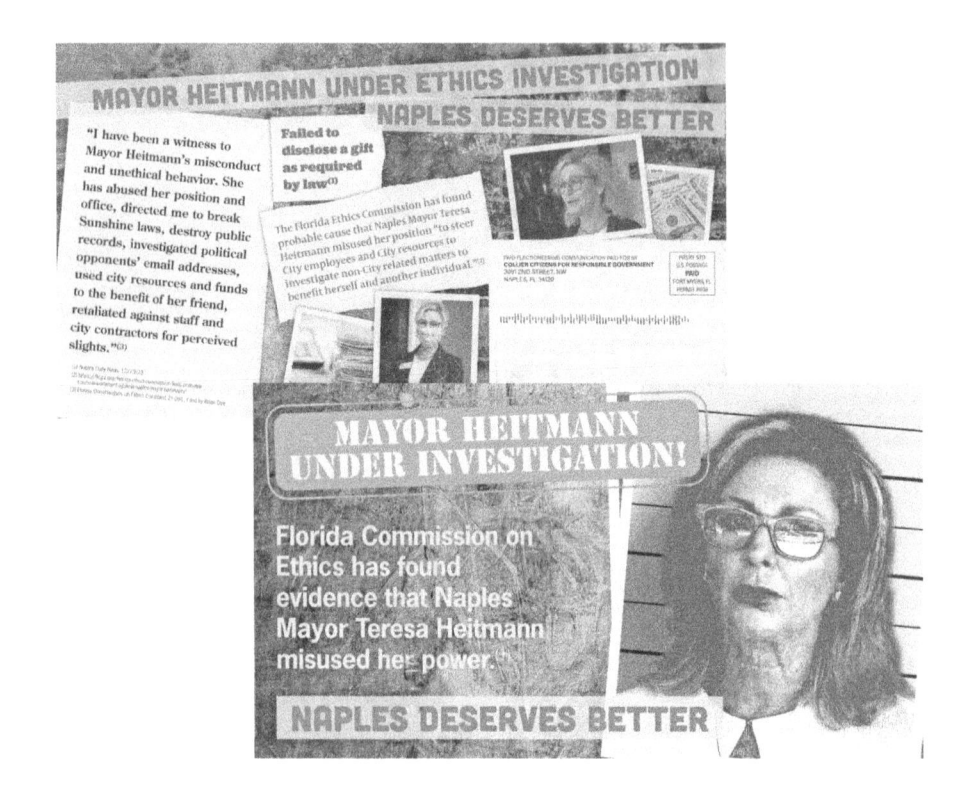

As public comment on the allegations swelled, it was reported that "Joe Karaganis, a Naples resident, said he was also a victim of the alleged hacking, and requested a 'thorough' investigation by the commission."[40] Karaganis had been involved in passing the charter amendment that created the local ethics commission and would later play a pivotal role in the 2024 city election.

Dye's complaint was followed by an accusation from former mayor Barnett that alleged Heitmann had accused him, along with Collier County Sheriff Kevin Rambosk, of running a child prostitution ring out of the Naples airport. Heitmann vehemently denied the charges and, after a phone call with the director of the Airport Authority and another with the sheriff, it was determined to be scurrilous.

The Dye complaint was passed up to the Department of Law Enforcement (FLDE) in Tallahassee. After finding her actions did not rise to the criminal level, FLDE told Dye's attorneys to bring it before the Florida Commission on Ethics, which later found possible probable cause, but it was marginal and never pursued.

Temporarily abandoning the negative, the PAC also pressed hard for a 4 – 3 voting majority on city council, using mailers to support the "team" as a group and each as individuals with specialized pieces laying out the same issues as Price: a reduction in taxes and traffic, choking down overdevelopment, protection of property rights, supporting law enforcement and first responders, preserving Naples' small city charm, and improving access to healthcare by moving to quickly approve the Heart and Stroke Center at the hospital.

Patriots with Principles

Another PAC working on behalf of Price and the "team," cranked up in 2023 and included a number of local heavyweights and state officials like former Ambassador and United States Representative Francis Rooney, Lutgert Companies chairman and Naples Community Hospital board chair Scott Lutgert, Sunshine Ace Hardware President Michael Wynn, and developer/architect Matthew Kragh.

Patriots was less visible than others. Its role was more to pay for campaign management and a massive TV schedule on Fort Myers channels and cable to promote Price as a warm and caring person showing him interacting with family and neighbors. The spots were well done and stayed away from issues and attacks.

Realtors® Political Advocacy Committee

Gary Price had on "the team" a real estate agent, Berne Barton. The PAC was involved in elections throughout the state, and the local Naples Area Board of Realtors® applied for support. And got it to the extent of $1,000 contributions to the Price slate along with two mailers, one supporting the "team" and the other supporting Price.

PAC fund reporting

The chart below reflects contributions and expenditures reported to the Florida Department of Elections from October 1, 2023, to June 30, 2024, or later if reported. However, it is a completely inaccurate reflection of the money actually spent because the reporting and timing of payments was always subject to money being quietly and quickly moved around.

PAC	CONTRIBUTIONS	EXPENDITURES
Citizens Awake Now	$22,977	$7,741
Win America	$55	$3,423
Collier County Citizens Values	$100	$1,857
Patriots with Principles	$175,750	$119,304
Collier Citizens for Responsible Government	$161,000	$154,869
Realtors Political Advisory Committee		
Accountability in Government Inc.		$5,725
Florida's Values	$45,000	$53,168
TOTAL	$404,882	$346,087

As shown above, although Citizens Awake Now mailed out at least eight pieces, expenses from October 1, 2023, to July 26, 2024, (above) amounted to a little under $7,800. Normally, a mailing piece to all registered voters in the city, including printing and postage, runs around $5,600.

In the case of Florida's Values, a PAC run by Stafford Jones, $35,000 in the reported expenditures is actually money moving between his PACs. In every one of the seven listed below, there are legal, accounting and filing fees that qualify as expenses to operate the PAC, so it's nearly meaningless attempting to pinpoint exactly where the money went.

Heitmann

Heitmann had no PAC support behind her. She used family for campaign management and served as her own treasurer. Her donor base consisted primarily of retired citizens and local businesses. Of her $1,000 donors, forty were retirees and twenty-two small business owners. Twelve were from out of town.[41]

She relied heavily on yard signs, social media, and emails. By March, as the drumbeat of negative advertising from the Price PACs increased, she began to strike back both by defending her record and by attacking his.

On March 3rd she disputed the Realtors® PAC piece which said: "In our darkest hour (following Hurricane Ian) Gary Price was there to pick up the pieces." Heitmann responded: "Mr. Price was not even on council at the time of the hurricane. His innuendo is disrespectful to our wonderful first responders, our city employees, our elected officials, and you our city manager, all of whom gave 1000% 24/7 and remained dedicated to residents who continue to

CITY OF NAPLES 2024

recover from the storm of the century. Now when Mr. Price tries to take the spotlight for a tragedy that our employees and first responders put their lives on the line for, I say ... enough." [42]

[Campaign mailer for Gary Price, Naples Mayoral Candidate, featuring "HONESTY ★ ACCOUNTABILITY ★ EXPERIENCE ★", checkmarks for "Protecting Our Rights," "Holding City Hall Accountable," "Supporting Our Local First Responders," and "ETHICAL LEADERSHIP WE CAN TRUST." Election Day: March 19, Early Voting: March 9-16. Alongside a "BREAKING NEWS — Hurricane Ian floods Naples, damages boats, cars, businesses, homes -Local 10 News, 11/29/22" clipping and the text "IN OUR DARKEST HOUR GARY PRICE WAS THERE TO PICK UP THE PIECES."]

Two days later, she sent an email with a picture of a large dump truck emptying money out onto the street, with the comment "Now outsiders/developers are dumping big money behind Gary Price to buy the election, reverse progress, and threaten our quality of life." Below the dump truck were two bar graphs, one alleging Price voted to approve variances 88% of the time, and the second that 87%

75

of his money came from local real estate and development industry and interests outside the City of Naples.

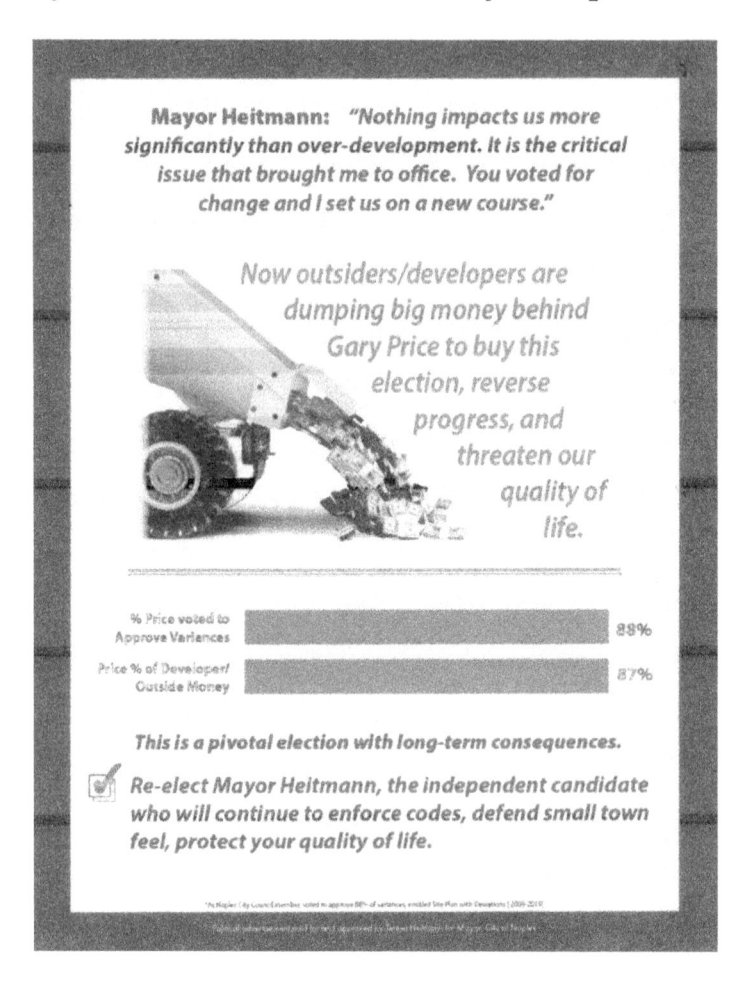

> **Mayor Heitmann:** *"Nothing impacts us more significantly than over-development. It is the critical issue that brought me to office. You voted for change and I set us on a new course."*
>
> *Now outsiders/developers are dumping big money behind Gary Price to buy this election, reverse progress, and threaten our quality of life.*
>
> | | |
> |---|---|
> | % Price voted to Approve Variances | 88% |
> | Price % of Developer/ Outside Money | 87% |
>
> *This is a pivotal election with long-term consequences.*
>
> ☑ Re-elect Mayor Heitmann, the independent candidate who will continue to enforce codes, defend small town feel, protect your quality of life.

Price vigorously disputed that second number during the entire campaign, but Heitmann stayed with it despite the fact that after she had first cited it at the League of Women Voters forum later donations reduced the amount reasonably attributable to contractors, developers, realtors and others.

Linda Penniman (redux)

Sick and tired of the drumbeat of negative campaign flyers and rhetoric on social media and the internet, and having been through two prior campaigns, Penniman decided, in late February with the frenzy of negative advertising coming from multiple PACs, to take the high ground. She did so by creating both a mailer and yard signs with a red traffic "Stop" sign followed by the message to "quit the dirty campaigning." It did little good because the outpouring of negative messages continued, but the demand for her yard signs increased dramatically and they began to populate more lawns.

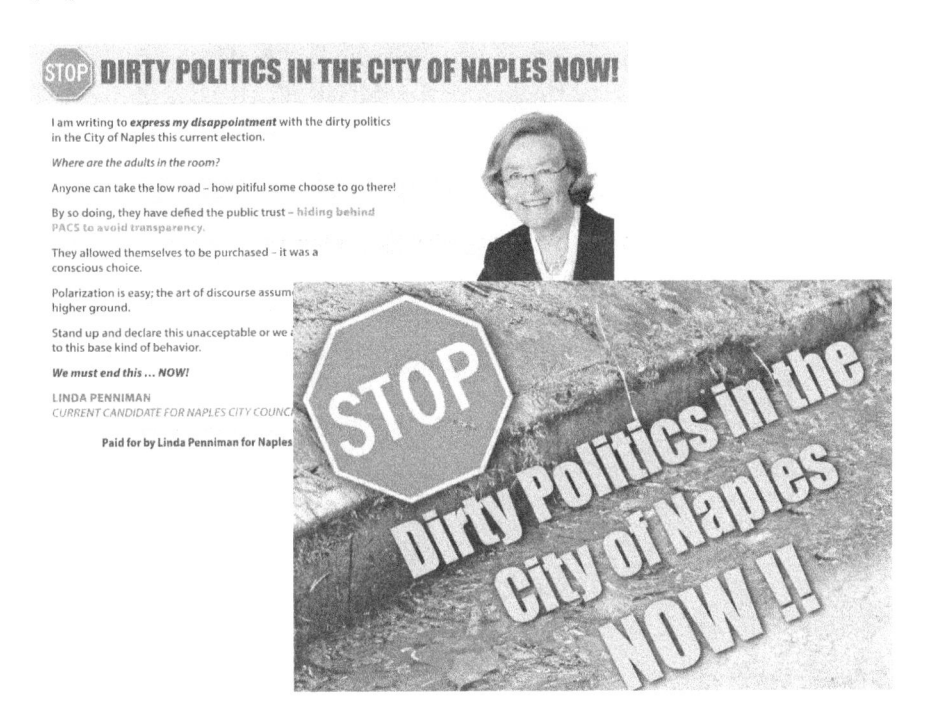

Facebook

Given the demographics of Naples, social media was regarded as a secondary means of communicating with the voters. However, one on Facebook stood out. Called GAP Stand, an acronym for Great American Patriots, it carried a post alleging that Gary Price was pro-abortion because of a vote in 2021 against the idea of creating Naples as a "sanctuary city" for the unborn.

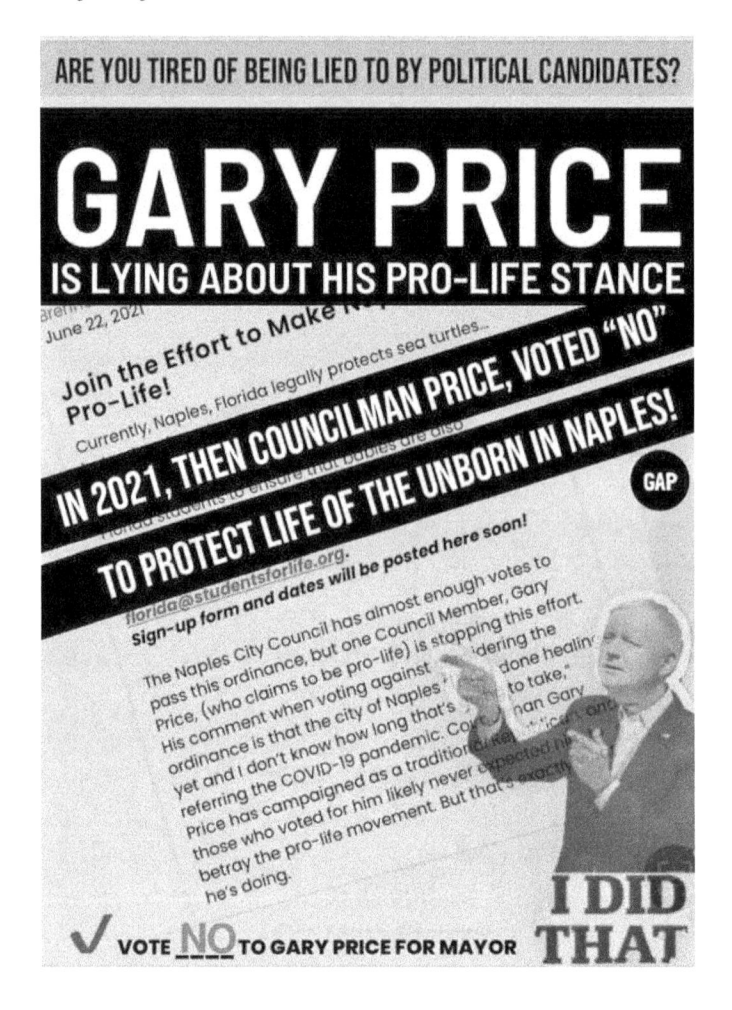

Another post listed a series of votes taken by Price supporting mask mandates, tax hikes, a decrease in police pay, and noted that 87% of his financial supporters were "developers and builders," closing with the final comment: "His heels are higher than his standards." In yet another, GAP Stand pointed out that Heitmann had marched with Black Lives Matter protesters on Fifth Avenue.

One quickly followed it, showing a male dog lifting his rear leg to irrigate a series of signs promoting Heitmann, Price, Barton, Perez-Benitoa and Kramer.

There was also posted on the site an ad for yard signs stating it was "paid for and approved by Ted Blankenship for Naples mayor." [43]

On its main Facebook page, GAP Stand listed 4,900 friends among whom was Bill Oppenheimer, a pro-life activist who ran for council for a short period until suffering an illness in 2021 and withdrawing from the race. Sitting

Vice Mayor Terry Hutchison was on the site as a "friend" and, not surprisingly, so was Matt Hurley.

Thoughts on PACs

Naples had never seen so much dark money funneled through PACs attempting to influence a local election. In 2024, it was driven partly by the secrecy afforded by the ability to report only after the polls closed, partly by no limits on the amounts contributed with the statutory limit of $1,000 to an individual candidate, and only slightly by the ability to quickly move money around with little oversight.

While preferring to not comment directly, Blankenship said this to the local press: "My entire campaign has been based on my record and my plans for the mayor's office," he said. "I have sent no messages of any kind disparaging my opponents. I find negative campaigning unproductive and frankly I believe the voters do not like it." [44]

Reflecting back on the election, Heitmann commented: "Debates and discussion among the candidates were always civil, but I was disappointed and hurt at what came about with the PACs. It was troublesome for me to make accusations with no facts behind them. With a couple of exceptions, I simply refused to respond to the nonsense. No one ever asked me about some of the misinformation contained in those mailers. It was all about the PACs and political strategists behind them, something that has been growing on the national level, but for the first time it became local. We don't need that here." [45]

"CHICAGO LITE"

☆☆☆

Joe Karaganis was a lawyer in Chicago who spent more than 50 years representing a wide assortment of state and local governments, environmental groups, and major industries in disputes involving natural resources throughout the United States.

Graduating in 1966 from the University of Chicago Law School as a self-described "idealistic liberal," he shied away from the Democratic machine politics that pervaded Chicago and Illinois government.

As a long-time observer of Chicago and Illinois politics, Karaganis was familiar with the backroom dealmaking where political insiders were given special favors—with sweetheart contracts that went to political favorites and honest competitors were shut out. Decisions on important government issues in Chicago were often made not on objective merits but on favoritism to political insiders.

Chicago's press observers cynically called this process "The Chicago Way".

Instead of joining the Democratic machine that ruled Chicago (or the weaker Republican political organization that often made insider deals with the machine), Karaganis carved an independent path. He served for many years as a bipartisan legal advisor on major environmental issues to both Republican and Democratic public officials—including several Illinois Attorneys General, Democratic Congressman Abner Mikva, Republican Henry Hyde, Chairman of the U.S. House Judiciary Committee, and numerous officials in Illinois and other locations throughout the country.

Karaganis became concerned when a real estate developer purchased a small parcel of land adjacent to his Naples home. The parcel was too small to meet the dimension limits of the city's code; nevertheless, the developer purchased the substandard lot knowing that the Naples City Council had been lax in enforcing the code granting numerous "variances."

Karaganis believed the developer had a special relationship with the then mayor, Bill Barnett, and had hired a prominent real estate lawyer to request a variance for the small lot. But, Karaganis alleged, this same lawyer was also serving as the mayor's personal attorney and had hired the mayor's daughter in his law firm, pointing out that this apparent conflict of interest was never disclosed to the public or the other members of the city council, and the mayor never recused himself from voting on project requests brought by his personal lawyer.

The result, in Karaganis 'opinion, was repeated approvals of controversial requests for zoning exceptions, deviations, and code amendments brought before the council by

Barnett's attorney. The situation got so bad that Karaganis—reflecting on Chicago's unsavory reputation as "the Chicago Way"—gave Naples the nickname: "Chicago Lite".

Concerned about a number of unreported and perceived conflicts of interest Karaganis became a board member and registered agent for Ethics Naples, a group established to successfully pass a city charter amendment in 2020 to create an ethics commission.

Karaganis was a Heitmann supporter in 2020, and again in 2024 when he became increasingly concerned with the negative advertising being heaped on her, and on Blankenship, by the dark money PACs. For weeks, he toyed with the idea of putting out an explanatory flyer to expose the PACs but hesitated because of his concern that it might hurt his preferred candidate.

Relying on his history and experience with Chicago politics, he drew parallels between the influence peddling there and Naples, tying Price to former mayor Barnett and referencing the undisclosed business relationship between Barnett and John Passidomo, the go-to lawyer in town—who also happened to have represented Karaganis' neighbor who wanted to subdivide into a non-conforming corner lot.

After toying with the piece and constantly editing, he decided to send it out with the title:

"For Sale in the March 2024 election: The Naples City Council."

Karaganis' mailer was sent to all registered voters in the city to be in mailboxes about two weeks before the election.

FOR SALE IN THE MARCH 2024 ELECTION: THE NAPLES CITY COUNCIL

BIG-MONEY REAL ESTATE DEVELOPERS AND THEIR FRIENDS ARE TRYING TO BUY CONTROL OF THE NAPLES CITY COUNCIL!

QUESTION: Can mountains of campaign cash — from big money real estate developers and their friends — buy the 2024 election for the offices of Naples Mayor and three Naples City Council seats?

Gary Price — who forged his political career by serving several years as protégé and right-hand man to former Naples Mayor (**Bill Barnett**) —certainly thinks so!

FOLLOW THE MONEY!

We are all familiar with the saying – "YOU CAN'T FIGHT CITY HALL".
But **Gary Price and his big-dollar real estate contributors** think "**YOU CAN BUY CITY HALL!**"

Campaign finance reports with the City Clerk show that a host of big-money real estate developers — and their friends and relatives — have already **poured over $200,000 into the campaign of Gary Price** (and his hand-picked **"TEAM NAPLES"** candidates for City Council) in the early days of the 2024 campaign.

He named major contributors to two PACs, Patriots with Principles and Collier Citizens for Responsible Government. Included in the Patriots were many of the major donors to the 2020 Citizens Who Love Naples PAC, including Fred Pezeshkan and Moe Kent, Phil McCabe, and Matt Kragh.

The concluding statement: "The questions for Naples's voters are stark and simple. Do we let a small group of mega-millionaires, big-money real estate developers 'buy' control of our Naples City Council—by massive funding of political candidates willing to let high-density developers ignore the protections of the Naples Code? Or do we say: Absolutely Not! The Naples City Council is Not for Sale."

It's difficult to assess the effect of the Karaganis mailer. It's likely there was minimal effect on absentee mailed ballots. Coming out just before early voting, which began March 9th and ran through March 16th, it was a close shave. For election day, March 19th, there was plenty of time for it to be considered.

The piece was unusual in many ways. Most donors, willing to spend five figures to influence an election, preferred to use dark money PACs. This was a single individual, not a candidate, producing a narrative that took no prisoners, named names, and was unapologetic in its blunt analysis. It ran to nearly ten pages whereas most mailed flyers attempted to make their point in as few words as possible combined with pictures and illustrations, but Karaganis' piece had only two small cartoons. It required careful reading.

Teresa Heitmann had mixed feelings about the mailer: "I knew about it but was against sending out the piece because I am always so concerned about hurting people. But what Mr. Karganis compiled was truthful and gave light to some hidden facts. Voters expressed to me personally that it gave them awareness that they didn't have before." [46]

In an election where twenty-two votes were the margin of victory, it's not presumptuous to believe that the Karaganis piece, because it was so unusual, may have had an important—and perhaps game-changing—impact on the 2024 City of Naples election.

THE RESULTS

☆☆☆

The polls in the city all closed on time, at 7:00 p.m. Marked ballots were packaged, sealed, and sent to the Supervisor of Elections office. Mailed and early ballots were already there, and a total of 21,077 paper ballots were stored, with 8,565 from the city, pending the result of the initial count.

Machine totals were transmitted electronically and at 7:56 p.m. preliminary and unofficial results were announced. Teresa Heitmann had bested Gary Price by twelve votes, 3,257 to 3,245. Ted Blankenship ran third with 2,044 votes. The slim margin was less than 0.5%, so a recount would be necessary.

Initial results had Bill Kramer winning with 4,277 and Linda Penniman second with 4,160, totals that put them both on city council for the next four years. The third-place contest was a squeaker, between two members of the "team," with Berne Barton having 3,677 and Tony Perez-Benitoa with 3,644. Nick Del Rosso and Garey Cooper ran a distant fifth and sixth. With a thirty-three-vote margin a recount would be needed, and the canvassing board agreed to meet on Saturday, March 23rd to take the next step.

In the 2024 election, the canvassing board had a slightly different makeup. The chair of the county commission, normally on the board, was Chris Hall but he had endorsed Ted Blankenship for mayor, and was disqualified. In his place was Michael McComas, a graduate of Ohio State University and member of the Everglades City Council. The board's chair was Judge Janeice Martin.

On Saturday at 11 a.m., the conference room, with a picture window where the two counting machines were highly visible, was jammed. Candidates were there with campaign advisers and lawyers. City Clerk Pat Rambosk was there to monitor the process. Since Heitmann's margin of victory was initially twelve votes, with eighteen provisional ballots Price's lawyers and advisers held out hope that they might flip the result.

The recount included mailed and early ballots, some of which had been disfigured by coffee stains, rips and torn corners, so as the machines whirred through the piles being fed in, they would kick out any questionable ballots for further review. The mayor's race had eight needing duplicates and the council race ten. There were 88 undervotes in the mayor's race and one overvote.

The city council race was completely different with 4,858 undervotes, over half the total city votes cast, indicating that some voters preferred only one or two of the candidates running. There were 27 overvotes not counted, but all had to be reviewed by a member of a six-person group of election workers, fully visible to the gathered spectators.

Before final certification, Price's lawyer was joined by Tim Guerette, running against Melissa Blazier for supervisor in the August 20th Republican primary, in requesting yet another recount of the eighteen provisional ballots. The request was denied since none of the ballots were cast in the city.

In the mayor's race, the recount changed totals very little. Heitmann picked up twelve votes and Price two, making it 3,269 to 3,247. The eighteen provisional ballots, even if all went to Price, would not change the outcome.

In the race for council, Kramer ended up with 4,285, Penniman with 4,171 and Barton with 3,686. Perez-Benitoa had 3,652, outside the limit for a second recount.

The only outstanding issue remaining was overseas ballots. None were received, so on March 29th at 5:05 p.m. the canvassing board certified the results, and the 2024 election went into the history books.

When discussing the recount, Blazier was highly animated "I knew that with all the outside money the election was going to create problems. We had the recount in this conference room we're sitting in right now. It was packed with people watching the machines do the work. It was hot and crowded. The air conditioning couldn't keep up with all the people, but I think we got it right the very first time. Once people come in here and see what we do and how we do it, there is a sense of security. That's not to say that there aren't going to be people critical of the process, but I think the State of Florida has overcome the reputation it acquired over 20 years ago with the 'hanging chads' and I think today that we are a model for many other states trying to emulate what we do." [47]

ACKNOWLEDGMENTS

☆☆☆

This book was written in the hope that it will expose the raw underbelly of an election in a small city of 16,529 registered voters. It was a microcosm of a larger reality—the prevalence of big money in politics.

I am indebted to a number of people who helped pull all the data and mailing pieces together, notable Sandy Parker. She has her own operation—www.sparkers-soapbox.com—and does a superb job of gathering information to pass along in a straightforward way, objective and without embellishment. Stacy Vermylen provided me with her collection of mailing pieces for scanning, supplementing those we had received. This was helpful because not all mailers went to all ZIP codes in the City of Naples. Melissa Blazier, Collier County Supervisor of Elections, was a godsend. She was always quick to respond to my questions, and her answers were always direct and easy to understand.

I tried to contact most of the people written about in the book, but not all were willing to be interviewed, so I had to rely on secondary sources to present, as best as possible, their side of some of the controversies.

My grandson, another Nick Penniman, wrote part of the chapter on PACs. A sophomore at Middlebury College, he is deeply into analysis of his generation's culture, with essays having appeared in both *The Nation* and *The New Republic*. My son, with his own organization in Washington—Issue One—and granddaughter, a digital genius involved in two political campaigns, both have comments on the back cover. And, of course, my wife was elected to Naples city council in March 2024. They all share my desire to diminish to corrosive effect of big money in politics.

This book has limited shelf life but I hope it reminds us of how PACs, replete with misinformation, downright lies and nasty memes, can poison an election. And—as you have read here—they don't always win.

ENDNOTES

[1] Zuck, Lila: Naples: A Second Paradise. The Collier County Historical Research Center, Inc., 2013. pp. 77-83.

[2] *Ibid.* p. 88.

[3] *Ibid.* p. 672.

[4] *Ibid.* p. 229

[5] *Ibid.* p. 347.

[6] *Ibid.* p. 354.

[7] *Ibid.* p. 526.

[8] *Ibid.* p. 566.

[9] *Ibid.* p. 567.

[10] *Ibid.* p. 751.

[11] *Naples Daily News*, March 7, 2016.

[12] *Ibid.*

[13] The simpler explanation might have been that the signs were in the right-of-way, which is prohibited.

[14] Naples Daily News, March 15, 2016.

[15] After the election, on June 10th, U. S. District Court Judge Melissa Damian issued a preliminary injunction saying that the legislation, S. B. 774 was not "... substantially related to the state's identified interests." www.orangeobserver.com/news/2024/jun/11/florida-financial-disclosure-law-blocked-by-federal-judge/

[16] Hurley, Matt: Memo to Interested Parties: Current State of the Race for Mayor of Naples, FL. January 6, 2024.

[17] It was eventually moved to a private venue,

[18] www.sparkers-soapbox.com/collier-county-commissioner-elections-district-4, July 21, 2022.

[19] *Wall Street Journal*, May 31, 2024.

[20] Lauststen, Lasse and Alexander Bor: The relative weight of character traits in political candidate evaluations. *Electoral Studies*, 49.10.1016/j.electstud.2017.08.001.

21 *Naples Daily News*, March 14, 2024.

22 *Ibid*, February 3, 2018.

23 *Ibid*.

24 "Prohibits counties and municipalities within 100 miles of Hurricane Ian or Hurricane Nicole landfall from adopting more restrictive or burdensome procedures to their comprehensive plans or land development regulations concerning review, approval, or issuance of a site plan, development permit, or development order before October 1, 2024. Additionally, such counties and municipalities may not propose or adopt a moratorium on construction, reconstruction, or redevelopment of any property damaged by Hurricane Ian or Nicole (effective upon becoming a law)." 2023 Bill Summaries—The Florida Senate (flsenate.gov).

25 *Naples Daily News*, February 2, 2024.

26 *Naples Daily News*, March 14, 2024.

27 *Naples Daily News*, March 9, 2020.

28 *Naples Daily News*, October 16, 2019.

29 Memo titled: To: interested parties, From: Matt Hurley, Southeastern Strategies: Current State of the Race for Mayor of Naples FL, January 26, 2024.

30 *Ibid*.

31 Author interview with Melissa Blazier, May 24, 2024.

32 *Naples Daily News*, February 20, 2024.

33 *Ibid*.

34 Author interview with Melissa Blazier, May 24, 2024.

35 FOX4 News: February 16, 2024. Coates was Richard Coates, the registered agent for the PAC.

36 *Naples Daily News*, February 20, 2024.

37 *Ibid*.

38 *Ibid*.

39 NBC2 News: February 15, 2024.

40 *Naples Daily News*, June 1, 2021

41 I am indebted to Sandy Parker and her blog, Sparker's Soapbox, for pulling this kind of data together.

[42] Heitmann email, March 3, 2024

[43] www.facebook.com/p/Gap-Stand-100075335587817/

[44] *Naples Daily News*, February 20, 2024.

[45] Author interview with Teresa Heitmann, August 20, 2024.

[46] Author interview with Teresa Heitmann, August 22, 2024.

[47] Author interview with Melissa Blazier, May 24, 2024.